Dimensions of Ethnicity

A Series of Selections from the
Harvard Encyclopedia of American Ethnic Groups

Stephan Thernstrom, *Editor*
Ann Orlov, *Managing Editor*
Oscar Handlin, *Consulting Editor*

PREJUDICE

THOMAS F. PETTIGREW
GEORGE M. FREDRICKSON
DALE T. KNOBEL
NATHAN GLAZER
REED UEDA

The Belknap Press of
Harvard University Press
Cambridge, Massachusetts
London, England
1982

Library of Congress Cataloging in Publication Data

Main entry under title:

Prejudice.

    (Dimensions of ethnicity)
    "Selections from the Harvard Encyclopedia of American ethnic groups"—
p. i.
    Bibliography: p.
    Contents: Prejudice / Thomas F. Pettigrew—A history of discrimination /
George M. Fredrickson and Dale T. Knobel—Efforts against prejudice / Nathan
Glazer and Reed Ueda.
    1. United States—Ethnic relations—Addresses, essays, lectures. 2. United
States—Race relations—Addresses, essays, lectures. 3. Prejudices and
antipathies—United States—Addresses, essays lectures. I. Pettigrew, Thomas
F. II. Pettigrew, Thomas F. Prejudice. 1982. III. Fredrickson, George M.,
1934— . A history of discrimination. 1982. IV. Glazer, Nathan. Efforts
against prejudice. 1982. V. Harvard encyclopedia of American ethnic groups.
VI. Series.
E184.A1P67   1982   305.8'00973   82–6185
ISBN 0–674–70063–5 (pbk.)   AACR2

Foreword

Ethnicity is a central theme—perhaps the central theme—of American history. From the first encounters between Englishmen and Indians at Jamestown down to today's "boat people," the interplay between peoples of differing national origins, religions, and races has shaped the character of our national life. Although scholars have long recognized this fact, in the past two decades they have paid it more heed than ever before. The result has been an explosive increase in research on America's complex ethnic mosaic. Examination of a recent bibliography of doctoral dissertations on ethnic themes written between 1899 and 1972 reveals that no less than half of them appeared in the years 1962–1972. The pace of inquiry has not slackened since then; it has accelerated.

The extraordinary proliferation of literature on ethnicity and ethnic groups made possible—and necessary—an effort to take stock. An authoritative, up-to-date synthesis of the current state of knowledge in the field was called for. The *Harvard Encyclopedia of American Ethnic Groups*, published by the Harvard University Press in 1980, is such a synthesis. It provides entries by leading scholars on the origins, history, and present situation of the more than 100 ethnic groups that make up the population of the United States, and 29 thematic essays on a wide range of ethnic topics. As one reviewer said, the volume is "a kind of *summa ethnica* of our time."

I am pleased that some of the most interesting and valuable articles in the encyclopedia are now available to a wider audience through inexpensive paperback editions such as this one. These essays will be an excellent starting point for anyone in search of deeper understanding of who the American people are and how they came to be that way.

Stephan Thernstrom

Contents

Prejudice

1

PREJUDICE

Definitions of prejudice abound. Prejudice, one aphorism asserts, is being down on something you are not up on. Prejudice, goes another, is a vagrant opinion without visible means of support. For Voltaire, prejudice was opinion without judgment. But, like "intelligence" and other conceptions adapted from popular usage, the scientific conception of prejudice is at once both narrower and broader than its popular meanings.

Prejudice is often used to refer to bias, partiality, or a predilection; in the law, to harm and injury. None of these meanings is retained directly by social science. Instead, there has been an expansion of the popular meaning of prejudice as "an opinion for or against something without adequate basis." Notice that this conception includes both irrationality ("an opinion . . . without adequate basis") and emotional evaluation ("for or against something"). It is in these spheres of human cognition and affect, or thinking and feeling, and their links to behavior that social science has broadened its conception of prejudice into a useful tool for understanding ethnic relations.

Definitions and Concepts

There are two critical considerations for a workable definition of prejudice. First, for the cognitive, irrational component, how can one determine what constitutes an "inadequate basis" for prejudiced attitudes? Was it "prejudice" that caused many Americans during World War II to hate Adolf Hitler and his Nazi party? If the attitudes are largely justified by "the facts," then Americans were not prejudiced. But how can "the facts" be evaluated? Obviously, no sharp distinction can be made between an "adequate" and an "inadequate" basis for negative group attitudes. This logical problem is not as serious in practice as it first appears, thanks to the cognitive distortions that typically characterize the phenomenon. Gross overgeneralizations signal prejudice. A hatred of Nazis generalized to all of the German people regardless of their participation in the Nazi party clearly represents prejudice. Such overgeneralizations, called stereotypes, mark many, though not all, antagonistic group attitudes.

A second point concerns the affective, feeling component of prejudice. Favorable prejudice is possible as well as hostile prejudice, as illustrated by a loyal member's sympathy toward his own group. But when we fail "to love thy neighbor as thyself," to exhibit "brotherly love," to accord to outgroups what we routinely accord to our own ingroup, some degree of negative prejudice is involved. Again, no sharp demarcation can be drawn between "positive" and "negative" prejudice. But social science has limited the concept to group antipathies.

Prejudice, then, can be thought of as *irrationally based, negative attitudes against certain ethnic groups and their members.* It is clearly a value-laden concept, for it is regarded as "bad" and "wrong" to be prejudiced. Thus, prejudiced attitudes violate two basic norms, one cognitive and the other affective—"the norm of rationality" and "the norm of human-heartedness."

The norm of rationality enjoins us to seek accurate information, correct mistaken notions, make needed qualifications and differentiations—in short, to be as rational as human limitations allow. Prejudice clearly vitiates this norm with its overgeneralizations, prejudgments, and a general denial of individual differences. The norm of human-heartedness enjoins us to accept other groups and individuals in terms of their common humanity, regardless of who they are and how different they may be. Virtually all major religious and ethical traditions invoke this norm, and in secular American thought it appears in "rooting for the underdog." With its hostility toward outgroups, prejudice also vitiates this norm.

Drawing on the thought of both Gordon Allport and John Harding, a more comprehensive definition can now be advanced: Prejudice against racial and ethnic groups is an antipathy accompanied by a faulty generalization. It may be felt or expressed. It may be directed toward a group as a whole, or toward an individual because he is a member of that group. Thus, ethnic prejudice simultaneously violates two basic norms—the norm of rationality and the norm of human-heartedness.

Many other terms relate to this view of prejudice. Thus, prejudgment and intolerance each refer to just one of the critical dual aspects of prejudice. *Prejudgment* involves a premature cognitive fix on a subject prior to examining the relevant evidence; it constitutes a violation of the rationality norm. *Intolerance* represents a rejection of outgroups because of their differences from the ingroup; it constitutes a violation of the human-heartedness norm. Similarly, *bigotry* refers to a zealous ingroup devotion and consequent rejection of outgroups. *Xenophobia* goes further; it involves a fear of and aversion to all who are seen as different and strange.

Ethnocentrism is another closely related concept. It refers to the unquestioned belief in the superiority of one's own ethnic group and the consequent inferiority of other groups. William Graham Sumner wrote that ethnocentrism is a view of one's own group as the center of everything, with all others scaled and rated with reference to it. Unlike racist notions of inborn, biological superiority, however, ethnocentric beliefs are founded upon notions of cultural superiority. In practice, however, biological and cultural explanations for group superiority and inferiority often merge, and the distinction between ethnocentrism and racism becomes blurred.

Recently, it has become fashionable in America to discuss two varieties of racism—individual and institutional. The first of these is like prejudice in that it is a phenomenon of individuals. But *individual racism* includes both prejudicial attitudes and discriminatory behavior, and is based upon the assumption of the genetic inferiority of the outgroup. Generally applied to the attitudes and behavior of white Americans toward black Americans, its superiority-inferiority claims of race can be traced back to Count Joseph Arthur de Gobineau's essay on the inequality of the human races in the mid-19th century. By contrast, *institutional racism* refers to the complex of institutional arrangements that restrict the life chances and choices of a socially defined racial group in comparison with those of the dominant group. Institutional racism refers to a society's social structure and not to individuals.

Discrimination is closely allied with this conception of institutional racism. Both operate on the societal level. Discrimination is basically an institutional process of exclusion against an outgroup, racial or cultural, based simply on who they are rather than on their knowledge or abilities. But this simple definition belies the difficulty that often arises in determining group discrimination in our society. The problem arises most sharply in realms that were not long ago considered private matters and are today under public regulation. Here personal preferences and social policy collide. Is, for example, an employer's nepotism—the granting of jobs or favors to relatives—just a family affair? Or is it an act of discrimination because it restricts the chances and choices of outgroup members who may be better qualified than the family members? A generation ago the societal answer was that it was clearly within the rights of employers to hire whomever they wished. Today, with the nation having come to realize the complexity of group discrimination, the answer is likely to be that many forms of nepotism do indeed involve group discrimination.

Prejudice and discrimination are by no means perfectly correlated; one without the other is not at all uncommon. But, obviously, the two are linked. Discrimination and institutional racism not only limit an outgroup's opportunities, but they are powerful and ever-present reminders that directly support prejudice and individual racism. Hence, anti-Irish and anti-Semitic attitudes not only led in the late 19th century to blatant discrimination against Irish and Jewish Americans, but the discrimination itself fostered negative attitudes. Prejudice does not operate in a social and institutional vacuum; it thrives in a contaminated environment of ingroup privilege and outgroup exclusion.

Prejudice, then, is distinguished by two principal components, each of which violates a widely shared cultural norm. In terms of the intellect it violates rationality standards, and in terms of the emotions it violates human-heartedness standards. Following is a discussion of these cognitive and affective components.

Cognitive Factors in Prejudice

Individuals survive psychologically in a chaotic universe, bombarded with more sensory stimulation than they can possibly process and use. They thus must strive to organize their environment and give it meaning by simplifying and packaging the incoming stimuli into readily useful information. This effort is made possible by an array of interrelated cognitive processes that usually function well. But, necessarily, in reducing the stimulus overload to manageable size, they can lead to characteristic errors in the selection, accentuation, and interpretation of sensory data. The relevance of these cognitive processes for prejudice is considerable. Rationality becomes a norm—a norm that is impossible to attain fully and consistently. The irrational distortions that comprise prejudice must therefore be viewed as grounded not in aberrant but in normal and necessary human processes.

Sensory inputs are organized basically through the use of

categories—broad clusters of items that are conceptualized under a single label (furniture, people, Swedes). By classifying incoming information within our categories, we render the world meaningful. But this process typically leads us to overestimate the similarity among items *within* categories and the differences between items *across* categories. This distortion is implicated in prejudice because ethnic groups themselves, like sex, age, and social class, are salient categories for organizing what is known about people. And once individuals categorize Chicanos, Asians, and blacks, they are likely to exaggerate the commonalities within these groups and overlook the human similarities and universals that bind the groups to each other.

Individuals also make categorical differentiations within their own ethnic group, but few if any among other groups. A Scottish American may consistently employ the Highlander and Lowlander distinction to judge his fellow Scots. As a descendant of Highlanders, he can explain away unfortunate aspects of Scots by assuming that they must be of Lowland origin. But he may fail to distinguish similarly within other groups. These distortions do not in themselves constitute prejudice, but they are the foundation upon which the cognitive components of prejudice are constructed.

The ethnic organization of much of the world furthers this categorization process. Ethnic categories help individuals to understand themselves and others, as well as the culture. Furthermore, there is social support for the use of these categories, since others also use them. The mass media advance this ethnic categorization process, often in its most destructive form. Many groups objected to the *All in the Family* television series for precisely this reason.

Language and labeling also heighten this process, since ethnic labels are particularly salient and influential. Gordon Allport called them "nouns that cut slices." "Koreans," "Cubans," and other ethnic labels of primary potency obscure other human characteristics by magnifying one attribute out of proportion to its significance. To know that a woman is an American Indian often overwhelms the equally important facts that she is also a lawyer, a resident of Chicago, and a former swimming champion. This phenomenon is enhanced further by the use of emotionally charged ethnic epithets, such as spic, chink, harp, or canuck; their use usually signals prejudice in its rawest form.

There is also a personality dimension to this categorization phenomenon. The use of dichotomous categories—the saved and the damned, the good and the bad, natives and immigrants—is particularly prone to irrational distortions leading to prejudice. Research demonstrates that prejudiced individuals of various ages are more likely to exhibit this "intolerance of ambiguity" than are equally intelligent, more tolerant individuals. This cognitive style of requiring greater definiteness is revealed by prejudiced seven-year-old children who are less willing to face uncertainty in solving problems and by prejudiced teen-agers who more often prefer structured situations and possess more rigid conceptions of sex roles. Striking evidence is provided also by an attitude item that has differentiated between the prejudiced and the tolerant in hundreds of tested samples: repeatedly, the more prejudiced tend to agree that "there are two kinds of people —the weak and the strong."

Stereotyping, a principal form of the cognitive distortions of prejudice, arises directly from these cognitive means of simplifying and rendering meaningful what our senses record. Defining stereotypes broadly as *the overgeneralization of psychological characteristics to large human groups*, the phenomenon emerges from the errors and biases of thought and perception common to everyone, rather than from any "faulty reasoning process" peculiar to prejudice.

The term "stereotype," taken from printing, was introduced in 1922 by Walter Lippmann. He thought of stereotypes as "pictures in our heads" that were acquired culturally rather than through personal experience. Social scientists have employed the concept to mean images of groups that tend to be simple, erroneous, acquired second-hand, and resistant to modification.

Blatant stereotyping is a common phenomenon. It was even more common before World War II. One famous study in the early 1930s found that Princeton University students agreed in their assignment of many traits: "Germans" were thought to be scientifically minded (72 percent) and industrious (65 percent), "Jews" shrewd (79 percent) and mercenary (49 percent), "Negroes" superstitious (84 percent) and lazy (75 percent). Many similar studies conducted throughout the world have since shown comparable results.

This prevalence of stereotyping suggests once again that this cognitive distortion is not unique to prejudice and arises from natural means of thinking and perceiving. Thus, stereotypes emerge from the process of categorization. They bring simplicity, order, and meaning by supplying packaged content to ethnic group categories. When an individual encounters a Finn, he or she can maintain cognitive order and even reinforce an erroneous image by employing the standard categorization mechanism. All Finns will be perceived as being more alike and similar to the stereotype than they actually are; simultaneously, an individual may tend to accentuate the differences between Finns and Swedes in order to maintain differential stereotypes of the two groups. So two people of different ethnic origins but equally intelligent are likely to be perceived as differentially bright according to the stereotypes of the two ethnicities.

Stereotypes are also readily available images of social groups, images that can be triggered by nothing more than the mere mention of group membership. The distinctiveness, salience, and extremeness of stimuli all contribute to the mental availability of an image, and all three often underlie the development of stereotypes. These stimulus characteristics can establish a negative stereotype without the slightest basis in reality. In what is called "illusory correlation," the co-occurrence of two distinctive, low-probability events can lead to a sharp overestimation of the frequency

with which the two rare events occur together. This phenomenon contributes to stereotyping. Consider the publicity
given by the mass media when a rare and violent crime is
committed by a member of a small ethnic group. Even
though there is no ethnic correlation over time with the rare
crime, it is likely that an illusory correlation between the two
is established in the minds of many people.

Another factor contributing to the process is that individuals tend to see outgroup members who appear to possess
the accepted stereotypes as particularly representative of
their group. The informational value of non-occurrences is
typically overlooked. Consequently, the numerous instances
of outgroup members who do not possess the stereotype are
less salient, and therefore less likely to be viewed as representative. For those who believe all Italian Americans to be
members of the Mafia, law-abiding Italian Americans are
simply out of view.

This bias toward noticing "positive" cases and ignoring
"error" cases may operate with greater force in everyday
perception than in the psychological laboratory. Rarely in
the "real world" is an individual privileged to know accurate
baseline data about the traits of entire ethnic groups. Furthermore, differential association contributes to the bias. Individuals know their ingroup better and have more contact
with its members. Thus, extreme instances among the outgroup are more salient, more available to memory, retro-
spectively overestimated, and more likely to be seen as representative of the outgroup. Group members who have more
contact with the outgroup are therefore less likely to stereotype them. White stereotypes of blacks in Chicago, for example, become more distorted with increasing residential distance from the city's black areas. And ethnic stereotypes are
used less by those English and French Canadians who have
experienced the most interethnic contact. Such contact leads
to a larger sampling of outgroup behaviors that acts to
counter stereotypes, though the conditions of the intergroup
contact are crucial.

Ethnic stereotypes also act as anchors, as initial starting points. And adjustments from these anchors are often insufficient. Bigots know that not *all* Irish are "quick tempered"; but insufficient adjustment from this anchor makes it difficult to demonstrate the opposite of a stereotypical attribute. Only a strikingly "exceptional" performance that contrasts sharply with the stereotype can keep from being assimilated to the stereotypical anchor. This process probably affects negative more than positive stereotypes, since an individual generally grants greater weight to negative than to positive characteristics in evaluations.

Contrasting traits are also involved in the particular items that are selected out to characterize a group; since contrasts provide strong stimuli, real differences between groups are likely to appear in the stereotypes each group has of the other. This tendency does not deny the possibility that stereotypes can emerge without any objective basis whatsoever. But it does make it likely that most stereotypes are exaggerations of actual differences between groups.

The objective basis of ethnic stereotypes has long been the subject of much debate but little systematic research. On the one hand, stereotypes can evolve in contradiction to the facts. Armenian-American laborers in Fresno, Calif., during the 1920s were commonly viewed as deceitful, dishonest, liars, and troublemakers; yet they appeared less often in court, applied less often for charity, and possessed credit ratings equal to those of other ethnic groups. On the other hand, widespread agreement across many groups concerning the content of ethnic stereotypes suggests that there is at least some validity for most stereotypes. Actually, a group's members generally characterize themselves in ways similar to their stereotype, though they usually place more favorable connotations on the agreed-upon traits ("sly" becomes "clever," "pushy" becomes "ambitious").

The "kernel-of-truth" possibility receives further support from the fact that two contrasting types of ethnic stereotypes emerge throughout the world in relation to the societal positions occupied by the stereotyped groups. In psychoanalytic terms, one type is rooted in superego concerns and the other in id concerns. Outgroups with superego stereotypes are seen as mercenary, ambitious, sly, and clannish. They are frequently merchants who are not native to an area—middlemen caught between the landed and the laboring classes like the medieval European Jews; the Chinese merchants of Malaysia and Indonesia are often called the "Jews of Asia," and the Muslim Indian merchants of East Africa the "Jews of Africa." Outgroups with id stereotypes are seen as superstitious, lazy, ignorant, dirty, and sexually uninhibited. They are groups found on the bottom of the social structure. In Europe, "guest-workers," Gypsies, and southern Italians are often targets; in the United States, blacks and Mexican Americans inherit the id stigma. This worldwide differentiation in ethnic stereotypes reveals some of their rationalizing function. And though often founded upon a "kernel-of-truth," stereotypes still qualify as irrational in their exaggeration, their absolutism, and their insensitivity to contrary evidence.

To achieve a stable, meaningful view of a changing world, an individual must determine the causes and implications of his or her actions and the actions of others. But in carrying out this cognitive task, another distortion is commonly created that has been called "the fundamental attribution error." Observers generally underestimate the force of situational and societal pressures and overestimate the force of a person's dispositions on his behavior. This tendency may not be purely a cognitive process, for it is probably enhanced in a society such as ours that places particular emphasis upon values of individualism.

The fundamental attribution error is easily demonstrated. In one experiment, subjects played a quiz game with the assigned roles of "questioner" and "contestant." Though the game allowed the "questioners" the enormous advantage of generating all of the questions from their personal stores of knowledge, later ratings of "general knowledge" were higher for the questioner. This dispositional attribution was made not only by the questioners and uninvolved observers, but especially by the disadvantaged contestants themselves. Note that the powerful situational force (the quiz game's format) is minimized, dispositional characteristics of the salient person (the questioner) are causally magnified, and role requirements (of being a quiz contestant) are not fully adjusted for in the final attribution.

Analogies to these experimental results in ethnic relations come easily to mind. Groups located predominantly in one particular occupation play a limited set of social roles. But others, and even many of the group members themselves, are likely to overlook the situational and role requirements and to misattribute their behavior to some assumed personal dispositions. Ethnic cues are frequently vivid and salient, while environmental cues tend to blend into the perceptual background. Even an all-embracing institution such as slavery was generally disregarded by white Americans, and black behavior was causally attributed to peculiar qualities about blacks themselves. This widespread tendency is often described as "blaming the victim." Here we see how ethnic stereotypes and causal misattributions are components of the same cognitive process that underlies prejudice.

This fundamental attribution error is extended and accentuated in intergroup perception. It has been shown that we typically grant our spouse and close friends the benefit of the doubt in our causal perceptions. For them, we attribute positive actions to dispositional causes ("She did it because she has a good heart") and negative actions to situational causes ("He only did it because he had to under the circumstances").

Granting members of another ethnic group the benefit of the doubt, however, is not so common. In what has been labeled "the ultimate attribution error," intergroup perceptions are more likely than intragroup perceptions to assume "the worst." In explaining acts that are perceived as antisocial or undesirable, outgroup behavior is more frequently attributed to personal, dispositional causes. Often these internal causes will be seen as innate characteristics ("They have a high crime rate because they are born thieves"). But when acts are perceived as prosocial or desirable, outgroup behavior is more often "explained away" in one of four ways. We can account for the stereotype violation in situational terms with role requirements now receiving attention ("Under the circumstances, what could the cheap Scot do but pay the whole check?"). Or we can ascribe it to motivation, as opposed to innate qualities ("Jewish students make better grades, because they try so much harder"). Or we can attribute the behavior to the exceptional, even exaggerated, "special case" individual who is contrasted with her group— what Allport called "re-fencing" our stereotypes ("She is certainly bright and hardworking—not at all like other Chicanas"). Or we can explain it away as simply luck ("It was just luck; they are too dumb to have won it on their own").

The human need to maintain cognitive stability and meaningfulness is the principal reason behind the natural human processes that lead to group stereotypes and misattributions. But these distortions can also rationalize our actions toward the outgroup. Stereotypes can justify categorical rejection or acceptance of an outgroup, and can even justify such systems of exploitation as slavery.

This rationalization function is not a necessary condition for stereotyping. Research subjects are willing to express stereotypes for a range of little-known ethnic groups toward whom they harbor no affective feelings whatsoever (for example, college students regarding Turks as "cruel" and Eskimos as "quaint"). However, when these cognitive distortions join with hatred to form prejudice, rationalization seems always present. Indeed, the causal order of the cognitive and affective components of prejudice is a major difference between the ways in which bigots themselves and social scientists analyze the phenomenon. Bigots regard their negative feelings as following logically from the contemptible traits of the outgroup. Social scientists believe that the negative feelings generally come first and lead to the justifying stereotypes. Evidence for the latter contention is provided by the fact that ethnic stereotypes turn either side of the coin into justification for outgroup rejection. The hated others are either too lazy or too industrious, too cold or too emotional, too stupid or too shrewd. Further evidence is supplied by reviewing the affective factors of prejudice.

Affective Factors in Prejudice

Many different emotions can underlie prejudice. Violating the norm of "human-heartedness" can result from fear and threat, or jealousy and envy; it can range from intense hatred to simple indifference and an absence of human sympathy. But most research on prejudice has concentrated on the single, friendly-hostile dimension.

Hostility toward outsiders is generally developed by the growing child well before the referent is learned. In an example of linguistic and affective precedence in learning, the emotional tone is acquired and attached to a label ("them," "white people," "Hungarians") before the referent of the label is learned. Allport calls this first developmental stage the period of *pregeneralization*. Later the child learns the referent for the established dislike and enters the second developmental phase of *total rejection*. All members of the designated outgroup are now repudiated; and virtually no aspects of the outgroup's stereotype are favorable. Still later the child begins to achieve adult-like differentiation. Exceptions are cited to give the appearance of reason and sympathy. These refrains are painfully familiar and usually entail the key conjunction, "but." "Some of my best friends are Jews, *but* I don't like them as a group." "I'm for everybody having a fair chance, *but* Puerto Ricans don't deserve good jobs."

Fear is often an important emotion in this developmental sequence. Children pass through particular periods of being fearful of strangers in general; parents and other socializing agents may invoke fear as a tool; and sometimes traumatic incidents link an outgroup with fear. More commonly, symbolic transfer of fear occurs. For instance, children fearful of getting too dirty or of the night's darkness generalize this to dark skin color and subsequent dislike of dark people. Recent research has shown a pancultural preference for light over dark, presumably derived from the worldwide fear of the night together with the association of daylight with fear reduction and need satisfaction. This early light bias among children can be transformed, through general cultural and familial influences, into color and racial biases.

Further insight into the emotional components of prejudice is achieved by considering the needs of the individual that are met by social attitudes in general and prejudice in particular. Three broad classes of vital functions have been distinguished: object appraisal, social adjustment, and externalization. In *object appraisal*, attitudes aid in understanding "reality." As societies change, the social consensus as to what constitutes "reality" shifts, and attitudes may shift accordingly. This is the function of cognitive order and meaning that was previously emphasized as the dynamic underlying the cognitive components of prejudice.

In *social adjustment*, attitudes help people conform to what is expected of them. For many who harbor prejudice, attitudes against outgroups are not nearly so expressive of deep-seated personality problems as they are socially adaptive in a prejudiced milieu. The bigotry of conformity requires prejudice as "a social entrance ticket." Bigots for whom the social adjustment function is paramount possess an antipathy only for those groups that it is fashionable to dislike, not outgroups in general. They follow the path of least social resistance, for they do not need to hate so much as to be liked and accepted by people important to them. Hence, as social change proceeds and what is expected by others is altered, conforming bigots shed their prejudice with relative ease. They continue to conform but the customs and norms that guide their beliefs and actions have changed.

Attitudes can also reduce anxiety by serving an *externalization* function. This occurs when an individual senses an analogy between the object of the attitude and some unresolved inner problem. One then adopts an attitude that is a transformed version of one's way of dealing with the inner, affective problem. People project their emotional problems onto the external world through particular social attitudes. If you have sexual problems, you may regard Latins as dangerously hypersexed. If you have problems within your conflict-ridden family, you may regard Jews as dangerously clannish. Externalization theories of prejudice derive directly from psychoanalytic thought, and have received the most research attention by psychologists. The most prominent are the authoritarian personality theory and the frustration-aggression hypothesis.

The personality dynamics of anti-Semites in the United States were intensively studied during the 1940s. A syndrome of personality traits, labeled authoritarianism, was discovered that consistently differentiated highly anti-Semitic individuals from others. Central to the syndrome is anti-intraception, the refusal to look inside oneself and the lack of insight into one's own behavior and feelings. Authoritarians refuse to accept their emotions and try to deny them. As children, authoritarians may have been punished frequently by stern parents, and in turn felt intense hatred for them. Unable to express these aggressive feelings for fear of further punishment, authoritarians find them threatening and unacceptable, deny them, and begin to project them onto others. If they feel hatred for their parents, they see hatred not in themselves but in the dangerous outside world.

Consequently, authoritarians typically convey an idealized picture of their parents as near-perfect. Generalizing this unrealistic view to include other authorities, they come to view the world in good-bad, up-and-down power terms.

They are outwardly submissive toward those they see as authorities with power over them, and aggressive toward those they see as beneath them in status. This hierarchical view of authority links directly with ethnic attitudes. High-status ethnic groups are respected, and authoritarians treat them with deference. But low-status ethnic groups are disparaged. Prejudice becomes for many authoritarians "a crutch upon which to limp through life." Lacking insight into their own inner feelings, they project their own unacceptable impulses onto outgroups whom they regard as beneath them.

The basic work on this personality syndrome has been extended by hundreds of research investigations conducted since the original study appeared in 1950. Fundamentally, *authoritarianism is a consistent style and orientation toward life* that permeates a range of attitudes. In addition to ethnic attitudes, it relates to political and economic orientations, traditional family ideology, nationalistic sentiments, social status concerns, even personal alienation. It also has implications for ingroup attitudes, for authoritarian Jews have been found to be strongly anti-Semitic and authoritarian blacks strongly anti-black. It also involves dichotomous thinking that leads to more rigid ethnic stereotyping.

Sweeping as this contribution is to our understanding of ethnic prejudice, some qualifications to the theory of the authoritarian personality are necessary. The enormous attention it has received has led to the neglect of the other major functions of prejudice—object appraisal and social adjustment. And analyses of prejudice emanating strictly from authoritarianism theory give virtually no attention to the critical situational and institutional contexts of ethnic relations and prejudice. Authoritarianism is closely related to breadth of social experience: the syndrome is most intense in narrowly constrained, provincial social settings.

Implications that right-wing politics and mental illness are involved with the syndrome also require qualification. The authoritarian style is often represented in far-left as well as far-right politics. Authoritarians may lack positive mental health, but they are apparently not any more likely to be hospitalized for serious mental disorders than equalitarian individuals. There is, however, an apparent difference in symptom selection: authoritarians appear more prone to paranoid symptoms, equalitarians to depression. In short, the authoritarian orientation toward life is often implicated in prejudice, but it must be understood as part of a narrowed social context and not as a reification of some particular political stance or mental health condition.

The frustration-aggression hypothesis asserts that *all aggression is preceded by frustration*. Fortunately, the converse is not true; there are sublimating alternatives to aggression for the expression of frustration. Though frustration is created by an inability to attain desired goals, aggressive behavior is frequently not directed at the agents that actually keep people from achieving their goals. Frustrating agents are usually older, stronger, more powerful, or protected by cultural traditions. So hostility often gets channeled onto approved, vulnerable objects, *scapegoats* that have little to do with the original frustration. This displacement-of-aggression principle is recognized in the adage about the boss who criticizes his employee, who in turn argues with his wife, who becomes angry with her child, who kicks the dog, who chases the cat, who finally takes it all out on an innocent mouse.

One famous study demonstrates how these mechanisms fuel prejudice. First, attitudes toward Japanese and Mexicans held by 31 young men working at a summer camp were measured. Later the men were frustrated by having to complete a series of lengthy tests when they wanted a long-awaited night out at the local theater. Then the same attitude measures were readministered. Just as expected, the camp workers as a group reported less favorable attitudes toward the Japanese and Mexicans. A control group that had not endured the same frustration did not change its attitudes. Though some hostility was directed at the researchers, the

Japanese and Mexicans—completely uninvolved in the frustrating situation—bore the burden of the workers' wrath.

Compelling as these results are, it should be noted that just as frustration does not always lead to aggression, so aggression is not always displaced. Sometimes the hostility is directed at the true frustrating source, and realistic conflict rather than displaced aggression is being expressed. Nor are all scapegoats weak and vulnerable. Usually, however, scapegoats bear some symbolic relationship with the frustration.

Highly prejudiced individuals are both more susceptible to frustration and more prone to display aggression following frustration. An interview study of World War II veterans noted that the prejudiced reported more frustration during their armed service, but actually had not been exposed to objectively more harsh conditions than the less prejudiced. Another study found that highly anti-Semitic college women increased their hostility toward an innocent peer when annoyed by an experimenter, while more tolerant women actually became friendlier.

To sum up, prejudice, like attitudes in general, can serve three important functions for the individual. It can lend meaning to the world; it can help an individual to adjust socially; and it can externalize an individual's inner problems —as shown in the research on authoritarianism and frustration-aggression. Yet prejudice, in conjunction with discrimination, can also serve an additional function at the societal level. Typically, prejudice and discrimination together act in concert to protect economic and political interests. Negative group attitudes can arise from competitive fears of marginal and vulnerable groups. More often, they are manipulated to reinforce the interests of those who seek or are already in power. Anti-Semitism has long played this role in Russia, and its manipulation in Nazi Germany made this societal function of prejudice particularly notorious. In America, anti-black racism arose to protect slavery, and anti-Chinese prejudice during "the Yellow Peril" era and anti-Mexican prejudice arose to protect the exploitation of Chinese and Mexican labor. This recurrent societal phenomenon raises the question of how prejudice is related to intergroup behavior.

Prejudice and Behavior

Since prejudice results from the simultaneous violation of the norms of rationality and human-heartedness, it can be understood in cognitive and emotional terms alone. But there may also be systematic implications for behavior. Is prejudice simply reflected in thoughts and feelings? Or do bigots lash out at the disliked outgroup? Here we are interested in violations of the norm of justice and fair play.

Four levels of increasingly negative intergroup behavior can be specified: verbal hostility, avoidance, individual acts of unfairness, and physical attack.

Verbal hostility is the mildest behavioral expression of group rejection. Many prejudiced people never go beyond this level; and unprejudiced people sometimes engage in this behavior rather than deviate from what is socially expected of them. Fortunately, most verbal hostility never sets off more extreme negative acts.

Even when inconvenient, many prejudiced people simply *avoid* the disliked outgroup. They "avoid a scene" and protect their prejudicial attitudes by refusing to interact. In his psychoanalytic interpretation of American racism, Joel Kovel emphasizes this behavioral consequence of anti-black prejudice and labels it "aversive racism." In contrast to "dominative racism" that "openly seeks to keep the black man down," aversive racism ignores black people, avoids contact with them, and, at best, is "polite, correct and cold in whatever dealings are necessary between the races."

In Kovel's terms, dominative racism has declined in the United States in recent decades, and aversive racism now describes more accurately much of the interracial behavior of prejudiced whites. This distinction can also be usefully applied to ethnic interaction more generally; it appears that aversive, avoidance behavior is far more common than the dominative conflict represented by the next two levels of reaction.

Typically, the aversive racist maintains a self-image of a tolerant individual, and often reveals little prejudice on a questionnaire. Some college students who report the most favorable attitudes toward blacks on a paper-and-pencil test of prejudice are more reluctant to interact with a black partner in an experimental situation than other students with moderately favorable attitudes. Their taped voices in the interracial interaction are judged colder and more condescending; they select joint tasks and chair placements that require more remote forms of interaction; and they claim to have fewer hours available for future sessions with their black partners.

Prejudice can lead to *individual acts of unfairness*, where bigots act unfairly toward members of the despised outgroup in ways they would rarely act toward ingroup members. The Los Angeles real estate agent who routinely shows Chicano clients only the poorest housing at inflated prices illustrates this acting out of prejudice. So does the rural Wisconsin gas attendant who serves last those cars he thinks are driven by American Indians. Note that these unfair acts, while expressing the prejudicial attitudes of the actors, take place within a larger societal milieu of group discrimination. Only the extremely prejudiced, the truly dominative racists, frontally act out their hostile feelings in the face of societal sanctions against such behavior.

Unfair treatment of outgroups also includes differentially failing to provide help in situations where help is indicated. Social psychologists have studied this phenomenon by setting up field experiments in realistic situations: a black or a white man "collapses" aboard a New York subway, a black or white motorist with "car trouble" dials "the wrong number" with his or her "last dime" seeking a garage, or a black or white woman drops her packages outside a supermarket.

Do bystanders differentially help these "victims"? The results generally support the view that the "subjects" in these real-life dramas often react differently according to the victim's race. In ambiguous situations, whites more readily define the situation with a black victim as one not requiring help, and consequently do not offer assistance. For example, "the wrong number" phone call may be terminated earlier for the black-voiced motorist before the relevant information can be provided. In clear situations, help is offered both blacks and whites, but it may be more perfunctory for the black victims. A few of the many dropped packages are picked up at the supermarket for the black shopper, rather than providing the complete help commonly granted the white shopper.

At times of heightened anger and unrest, prejudice can lead to *physical attacks* against members of a hated outgroup. Sometimes this extreme form of acting out is carried out by individuals, as in the bar fight over an ethnic slur or the lone assassin who kills the highly visible leader of the outgroup. But ethnically directed physical attack is so extreme a response, even in relatively violent America, that it generally flares up only after group mobilization has taken place first. When churches or synagogues are desecrated, or homes of "invading" outsiders are damaged in an ethnic neighborhood, the attack is almost always the work of organized groups. Although all acting out of prejudice is shaped by the social situation, physical violence especially reflects the larger societal context.

The social mobilization for interethnic violence is even more necessary for the ultimate in prejudiced frenzy—the attempted extermination of the hated outgroup. The pages of world history of even the past century record a depressing number of these tragic genocides: the anti-Jewish pogroms of Russia in the late 19th century, the Turkish massacre of the Armenians during World War I, the Jewish Holocaust of World War II. The pages of U.S. history have their own stains—massacres of Indians—as at Wounded Knee in 1890, and over 4,700 recorded lynchings of blacks since 1881.

Individual prejudice of varying intensities joins with cultural traditions to prescribe certain kinds of interaction with the outgroup and to proscribe others: this is called *social distance*. "I will buy with you, sell with you, talk with you, and so following," Shakespeare has Shylock say to Bassanio in *The Merchant of Venice*, "but I will not eat with you, drink with you, nor pray with you." Buying, selling, and talking with a Christian were within the allowable limits for Shylock, but the more intimate relations of eating, drinking, and praying violated his sense of social distance. This concept has been measured since the 1920s by a paper-and-pencil questionnaire that asks respondents if they would "willingly admit members" of various groups: "to close kinship by marriage; to my club as personal chums; to my street as neighbors; to employment in my occupation; to citizenship in my country; as visitors only to my country; would exclude from my country."

Emory Bogardus first used this measure a half century ago to gauge the attitudes of nearly 2,000 Americans throughout the country toward 40 racial, religious, and nationality groups. He found an amazingly consistent pattern of group preferences across the nation. The least social distance was accorded the British, native white Americans, and Canadians; next came the French, Germans, Swedes, and other western and northern Europeans; then the Spaniards, Italians, and Jews and other southern and eastern Europeans; and, finally, the greatest social distance was accorded blacks, Japanese, Chinese, Hindus, and Turks. This pattern varied little with the respondents' region, education, occupation, income, or even ethnicity. Lower-ranked groups shared the pattern, save for placing their own group at or near the top. It is this consistent pattern of reported social distances, together with the evidence of the authoritarian personality and the persistent group stereotypes noted earlier, that makes it useful to retain the concept of prejudice as a general factor.

The Bogardus Social Distance Scale has been employed in investigations throughout the world during the past two generations. These additional studies lend further support for the utility of the social distance concept. One study introduced for ratings the names of three fictitious groups—the Daniereans, Pireneans, and Wallonians; and the subjects who rejected most actual outgroups also tended to reject these fictitious groups as well. This finding points up the contribution of individual prejudice to the social distance phenomenon; other findings on children point up the contribution of cultural traditions. By early adolescence, American children of various ethnic backgrounds yield a social distance rank-ordering of groups that is essentially the same as that found among adults.

The importance of culture is further underlined by research on the social distance attitudes of German, Japanese, and American students. German students reported occupation as the most important single characteristic governing social distance, followed by religion, race, and nationality. For the Japanese students, the social distance ordering was occupation, race, nationality, and religion. For the American students, race—the "American dilemma"—was the most critical factor, followed by occupation, religion, and nationality. Social class, as represented by occupation, played a significant role in the responses of all three countries. Indeed, social class is intertwined with ethnicity in the stereotyped imagery of the prejudiced individual. Thus, with no class information available, many Americans assume, for example, that an "Englishman" must be upper-status and Hispanics must be poor and lower-status, and these class identifications greatly influence their group stereotypes.

Discrimination has been defined as an institutional process of outgroup exclusion on grounds of birth. So defined, discrimination operates at a different level in ethnic relations from that of prejudice. As a social process, it is not merely the sum of all of the individually unfair acts perpetuated by bigots; prejudice and discrimination are only moderately associated, and one without the other is not at all uncommon. Clearly, one supports the other: prejudice legitimates discrimination, and discrimination breeds prejudice. Yet much discrimination is not the direct product of prejudice; it often results as an unintended result of institutional arrangements designed for other purposes. One investigation of manufacturers in Texas found no relation whatsoever between their racial attitudes and their actual practices for hiring black workers. Intended or not, however, the damage to the outgroup victims is the same.

Similarly, prejudiced people do not necessarily engage in the discriminatory process. Societal restraints and situational demands often override the impulse to act out individual prejudice. Consider a group of white steel workers in Indiana studied by D. C. Reitzes in the 1950s. These men were members of the same thoroughly interracial union and worked in interracial plants. Only 12 percent evidenced "low acceptance" of blacks in this work situation; and the deeper the involvement in union activities, the greater was their acceptance of blacks as coworkers. But neighborhood acceptance was a vastly different matter. Bolstered by a neighborhood organization that opposed desegregation, 86 percent of the white steel workers rejected the idea of allowing blacks to live near them, with those men most enmeshed in the life of the neighborhood evincing the most adamant opposition. The effects of harmonious interracial patterns in employment did not extend to housing, for no relationship existed between acceptance of blacks as fellow workers and acceptance of them as neighbors.

The key to understanding this situation is the operation of the organizations in each of the realms. Most of the steel workers conformed less to their personal prejudices than to what was expected of them in the two situations. Their inconsistency of behavior was more apparent than real, for in each instance most of the workers lived by the norms of the groups to which they referred their behavior. These reference-group norms often act in modern American society to produce what appear to be inconsistent ethnic patterns, to restrict the generalization of contact-induced attitude change from one institution to another, and to overwhelm the behavioral tendencies generated by ethnic attitudes. In this instance, prejudiced workers generally accepted blacks as coworkers along with the rest of their union, and tolerant workers generally rejected blacks as neighbors along with the rest of their coresidents.

Prejudice and Current Ethnic Relations

Virtually every American ethnic group has its own story of hard times and difficulties in becoming established in the New World. Though sharpened by their retelling over the years, these stories contain considerable truth. There has, in fact, been widespread ethnic conflict throughout American history, with both prejudice and discrimination pervasive. Racial conflict has been the most severe, followed by religious conflict. These conflicts have been in full view; American society has not tended to hide or deny them. Just the reverse of Latin Americans, people in the United States often deny social class problems, but employ ethnic conflict explanations even when inappropriate.

Data collected over the last three decades, whether concerning stereotypes or social distance, point to a single conclusion: prejudice in all of its measured forms appears to have slowly receded since World War II, though considerable prejudice is still found against some groups.

Research on stereotypes that was conducted in 1933 at Princeton University was repeated in 1951 and 1967. In the later experiments many more students objected to the task, and most stereotypes had both faded in intensity and become more favorable. In 34 years, many traditional stereotypes had waned: the sly (from 29 to 6 percent), superstitious (34 to 8) Chinese; the stolid (44 to 9), scientifically minded (78 to 47) Germans; the witty (38 to 7), pugnacious (45 to 13) Irish; the musical (32 to 9), artistic (53 to 30) Italians; the shrewd (79 to 30), mercenary (49 to 15) Jews; and the lazy (75 to 26), superstitious (84 to 13) blacks. Stereotyped images re-mained, but often assumed a more positive cast. The grasp-ing (34 to 17) Jewish image had evolved into an ambitious (21 to 48) one. Evidence of a similar trend for the entire adult population comes from national surveys. For example, only 42 percent of white respondents in 1942 answered "yes" to the question: "In general, do you think Negroes are as intel-ligent as white people?" By 1946 this figure had risen to 52 percent, and by 1956 to 77 where it has remained.

Recent American research on social distance reveals com-parable shifts. While the group rankings remain similar to those of the 1920s, the amount of social distance reported for the middle-range (southern and eastern Europeans and Jews) and the lower-range nonwhite groups has declined markedly. Hence, the overall pattern is still maintained, but the differences in reported social distances between groups has significantly narrowed over recent years.

But can survey data, in an age of aversive racism, reflect "real" change? Do these data not tell more about shifts in what is considered respectable verbal behavior than shifts in prejudice itself? Of course, even shifts in verbal behavior are not unimportant and have positive implications for ethnic relations. But there are reasons to believe that these data sig-nify more basic changes in prejudice as well. First, rapport in the survey situation is generally far closer than those un-familiar with the technique realize. Second, the remarkable consistency of these attitude trends extends to a wide variety of groups, questions, and survey agencies. Third, predic-tions of the 1960 presidential election, based on a single question exploring willingness to vote for a qualified Roman Catholic for president, proved quite accurate. Finally, the most compelling reason for accepting the validity of these survey data is the fact that the diminution of prejudiced re-sponses is consistent with the marked erosion in discrimina-tion in U.S. society over these same years. It is consistent, too, with the reduction in ethnic stereotyping in the mass media. To be sure, there remains considerable discrimination in American life and media stereotyping continues, just as surveys still reveal considerable prejudice. But all three phenomena have receded during the past three decades in a mutually reinforcing manner.

These trends challenge the conventional wisdom about prejudice as voiced by such diverse personages as former Senator George Aiken and Frederick the Great. "If we were to wake up some morning and find that everyone was the same race, creed, and color," Aiken argued, "we would find some other causes for prejudice by noon." Frederick the Great agreed: "Drive out prejudices by the door, they will come back by the window." Are, then, these trends of recent years merely fluctuations around a persistent phenomenon? Is prejudice always to be present?

Addressing this question requires a choice between two contrasting conceptions of aggression. Sigmund Freud postulated a closed system containing a fixed amount of instinctive aggression which, if not released through one outlet, will seek and find another. According to this "steam boiler" view, society must find a way in which to channel aggression through appropriate safety valves; otherwise, the reduction of one prejudice will merely surface as an increase in another.

By contrast, Gordon Allport proposed an open-system, feedback conception. Rather than a finite force that demands release, aggression for Allport is a variable capacity whose expression is governed by both internal and external conditions. From this vantage point, present trends in group attitudes are not at all surprising. Widespread group prejudice is not inevitable; and greater tolerance of one group improves the chances for greater tolerance of others.

The evidence for choosing between these rival models is not conclusive, though Allport's open-system view receives support from both cross-cultural and laboratory research. But both the open-system conception and research on attitude change underline the importance of institutionalized group protections in American society. Indeed, the trends since World War II are products of the slow, structural process of evolving institutional safeguards that provide the necessary external conditions for the reduction of prejudice. Many of these safeguards also provide the setting for subsequent changes in the behavior of individuals. And behavior changes, in turn, produce the internal conditions for reducing prejudice. These protections have evolved in various ways. Sometimes they emerge dramatically, as with the Civil Rights Act of 1964. More frequently, they develop without national attention, as with the entrance of Jews into engineering and Slavs into prominent political posts. They take shape in cross-ethnic political coalitions and lowered barriers to opportunity. Taken together, these protections erode the foundation of group discrimination.

Institutional safeguards that go beyond mere restraint and prompt new intergroup behavior act to reduce prejudice directly. This process, too, contradicts conventional wisdom. It is commonly held that attitudes must change before behavior; yet social psychological research points conclusively to the opposite order of events as more common. Behavior changes first, because of new laws or other interventions; individuals then modify their ideas to fit their new acts.

The future of group prejudice in the United States cannot be foreseen apart from its social and political contexts. Although institutional safeguards developed in recent decades have been instrumental in reducing prejudice, there is no guarantee that they will be maintained, much less furthered. The retrenchment of the 1970s makes this lesson clear. But these institutional protections were largely achieved by the most self-identified races and ethnic groups, and efforts to advance them will probably be reinstated in some later, more propitious era. To be sure, ethnic loyalties themselves require group pride, even ethnocentrism; prejudice as a phenomenon will not vanish, but institutional constraints can reduce it and restrain its negative effects on American society. In this important sense, we can concur with Thoreau that "it is never too late to give up our prejudices."

2

A HISTORY
OF DISCRIMINATION

Much of the history of intergroup relations in the United States is a record of prejudice and discrimination against those considered racially or culturally inferior by a dominant or majority element. The minimum qualifications for membership in the privileged majority have been a white skin and European ancestry, but these attributes by themselves usually have not been sufficient to guarantee unfettered access to the core institutions of the society. The intense Protestantism of the original British colonists helped establish a long tradition of discrimination against Roman Catholics and Jews. At times there have been efforts to make the core group not merely white and Protestant but also "Anglo-Saxon." Hence neither majorities nor minorities, neither discriminators nor their victims, can be regarded as absolute and fixed entities. The complexities of American pluralism have even made it possible for members of some groups to be "in" and "out" at the same time; "in," for example, as whites licensed to discriminate against blacks, but "out" to the extent that their religious and cultural characteristics prevented their full acceptance by an Anglo-American elite.

Prejudice and discrimination are closely related but clearly distinguishable phenomena. Prejudice can be defined as an attitude of generalized hostility or aggression against a group of human beings who are thought to have some undesirable characteristics in common. It manifests itself in such ethnic stereotypes as the lazy Negro, the drunken Indian, the unscrupulous Jew, or the unruly Irishman. Prejudice may have its source in the personality disorders of bigoted individuals or it may be a manifestation of conformity to group norms. The latter type is of principal interest to historians and sociologists because it usually reflects an established pattern of ethnic inequality. Discrimination, on the other hand, refers to actions that serve to limit the social, political, or economic opportunities of particular groups. When such actions become institutionalized through either law or custom they result in substantial inequities in group access to wealth, social status, and political power. Discrimination may appear to be simply the acting out of prior prejudice, but there is evidence to suggest that prejudice becomes fully developed and formally sanctioned only *after* the process of differential treatment is well under way. Attitude and action tend to feed on each other, creating a vicious circle that works to enhance the power and prestige of one group at the expense of another.

Specific American minorities have experienced this vicious circle in differing ways and to varying degrees, and the historical pattern is complicated further by the changes that have occurred over time in the situation of each group. One way that the special circumstances affecting the fate of particular ethnic groups can be placed in a comparative perspective is by referring to three main variables that contemporary sociologists have found at work in all cases of "ethnic stratification." The first of these is *ethnocentrism,* a basic feeling that "we" are different from "them" in ways that make "us" better than "they" are. The intensity of ethnocentrism is determined in large part by prevailing notions of how substantial and enduring these group differences really are. To the extent that the differences are considered innate or "racial," prejudice tends to be accentuated and discrimination is likely to be more rigid and systematic. A second source of variations in attitude and treatment is the relative strength of the *incentive* for degrading and subordinating a particular group. The need for an exploitable labor force or the desire to gain an advantage in the competition for some scarce resource, such as land or industrial jobs, can be powerful motives for ethnic discrimination, but such material incentives are not constant and will vary in response to larger patterns of economic and social development. Finally there is the factor of the actual *power* differential between the groups involved. Ethnocentrism and economic interest can lead to the dominance of one group over another only to the extent that the former has the physical ability to impose its will on the latter. If group vulnerability invites oppression, any substantial increase in the material or cultural resources of a victimized group should tend in the long run to improve its social position and increase the rights and opportunities of its members.

For purposes of analysis, the principal victims of prejudice and discrimination in American history can be divided into five categories. First are the indigenous peoples conquered during the process of Euro-American colonization and territorial expansion, namely the American Indians. Next to appear on the scene as objects of domination and exploitation were the involuntary immigrants from Africa, originally imported mainly as a source of slave labor on the plantations of the colonial South. The newcomers from Asia who arrived on the West Coast during the 19th and early 20th centuries form a third category. In a unique fashion, the Chinese and Japanese shared with Afro-Americans some of the disabilities associated with race and color while at the same time retaining an integrated culture that differed substantially from that of the Euro-Americans. A Spanish-speaking or Hispanic minority was created first by the absorption of Mexicans that accompanied the westward expansion of the United States in the 19th century and then by the subsequent immigration of Mexicans, Puerto Ricans, and Cubans. The members of this fourth ethnic category have been distinguished from "Anglos" not only by language and culture but also, in some instances, by the racial characteristics resulting from a background of intermixture with Indians or blacks. The fifth and largest grouping resulted from the massive migration in the 19th and 20th centuries of Europeans with cultural and social attributes that conflicted with the Anglo-American norm. These white "ethnics" usually suffered prejudice and discrimination in more subtle and less formalized ways than Indians, Afro-Americans, Asians, or Hispanics but they were nevertheless vulnerable to some forms of economic exploitation and were, at least for a time, treated as "strangers in the land" without a full claim to the rights and privileges of those who considered themselves charter members of the United States.

There are several smaller groups that might be included by a slight stretching of each of the five categories: Eskimos, Aleuts, and Hawaiians among the indigenous peoples; black West Indians among those of slave descent; Filipinos, Koreans, and Vietnamese as part of the Asian group; South Americans of various nationalities under the Hispanic category; and Middle Eastern immigrants, especially Syrians and Lebanese, as part of the white ethnic population. But each of these groups has had its own special experience with prejudice and discrimination, and limitations of space and information preclude their inclusion in this survey.

American Indians and the Burden of White Ethnocentrism

The descriptions of American Indians available to prospective English colonists in the early 17th century provided no sure guide about how these indigenous peoples should be treated or how they might contribute to the success or failure of a European white settlement. Most voyagers and explorers had described the "savages" of the New World as living and behaving like wild beasts and had raised doubts as to whether they were fully human. But another opinion, carefully nurtured by some of the promoters of colonization, held that they were natural men, living in primal innocence, who had a gentle and tractable nature that made them obvious candidates for Christian conversion and eventual assimilation into a civilized community. If the former image implied segregation or extermination, the latter envisioned coexistence in the same society, although not necessarily on an egalitarian basis.

On the surface at least, the official ideology of the colonizers of Virginia and New England was strongly assimilationist. The letters patent setting up the Virginia companies of London and Plymouth in 1606 stressed the conversion and civilization of the natives as a prime motive of settlement, and missionary work was much discussed and sometimes undertaken in the early years of colonization. Considerable sums were raised for the purpose in England, and in Massachusetts there was a substantial effort to organize the red heathen into Christian communities. One need not doubt the sincerity of these endeavors to explain their failure. Seventeenth-century colonists did not give up on the Indian because they regarded him as racially inferior and innately incapable of civilization, but they did despise Indian culture and especially Indian religion, which they regarded as worship of the devil. Consequently, the Indian could become a "civilized" man only by divesting himself of everything that made him an Indian except his tawny complexion. The demand that they commit cultural suicide and subordinate themselves socially and politically to the European colonists was deeply resented by most Indians, but even more threatening was the spread of white agricultural settlement into their hunting grounds. In Virginia the Indian reaction came quickly in the form of an uprising in 1622 which wiped out approximately one-third of the colony. In Massachusetts the major explosion did not occur until 1675 when Metacom (King Philip) led a confederation of tribes in a last desperate effort to drive the Puritans into the sea. The crushing of these Indian rebellions against white encroachment and cultural imperialism brought an effective end to the assimilationist program and the hopes for Indian incorporation into the colonial communities. The new tendency to regard all Indians as permanent outsiders was manifested during King Philip's War in the unprovoked attacks by Massachusetts colonists on the "praying Indians" who had accepted Christianity and remained loyal to the whites.

It was in the wake of 17th-century Indian wars that the policy of assigning defeated or debilitated Indian tribes to a separate existence on reservations was first adumbrated. Virginia inaugurated a reservation system for tidewater tribes that were being outflanked by white settlements in 1653, nine years after a second massive Indian uprising had been suppressed. In New England the establishment of separate towns for Christianized Indians antedated King Philip's War but the policy of settling weaker tribes on small reservations was accelerated after the defeat of Metacom and his allies. The reservation system, which was to constitute the essential matrix of future relations between whites and subjugated Indians, was in part an act of mercy providing some chance for the survival of Indian communities. But it was also an act of rejection, a form of apartheid, signifying that whites preferred to isolate tribal remnants in peripheral areas rather than attempt the difficult task of intermingling whites and Indians within a single community.

Yet the very fact that Indians were not incorporated into white society probably saved them from direct economic exploitation. Red captives were sometimes enslaved in the colonial period, especially in South Carolina early in the 18th century, but the greater availability and suitability of black Africans for plantation labor brought an early end to Indian servitude. The whites wanted the Indian's land, but they neither needed nor desired his labor. Consequently, Indians as a group were not saddled with the slave stereotype of the lazy, hapless, and docile dependent.

Because of his relative isolation from white society there remained about the Indian an aura of dignified self-reliance that made it possible for some white Americans to romanticize his character. The cult of "the noble savage" may not have been transplanted in all its purity from the salons of

Paris, but, beginning in the late 18th century, it did have some effect on American thinking about the real "savages" on the frontier. Intellectuals like Thomas Jefferson, responding to European attacks on the allegedly debilitating effects of the American environment, defended the Indian as a superior physical specimen. Furthermore, the Enlightenment belief in the virtues of natural man and the existence of an innate moral sense suggested that Indians might serve as exemplars of uncorrupted human nature. Yet few white Americans seriously questioned the beneficence of the westward march of "civilization." Indian virtues, it was determined, were "savage" virtues worthy of admiration, but distinctly inferior to the higher virtues of "civilization." Hence the conception of savage nobility was absorbed into a theory of social progress that posited the inevitable disappearance of precisely those qualities that gave the Indian a certain dignity. However, philanthropic opinion in the age of Jefferson did not believe that the Indian himself was necessarily doomed, even if his way of life was an inevitable casualty of social evolution. The general assumption seemed to be that a noble savage might also be an apt candidate for "civilization." Thus the massive dispossessions and removals of the tribes west of the Appalachians in the period between 1790 and the 1830s were accompanied by insistent claims that the ultimate goal of white policy was the eventual absorption of individual Indians into Euro-American society. Money was appropriated by Congress for this purpose, and government agents and missionaries cooperated in efforts to bring a combination of Christianity, literacy in English, and agricultural technology to as many of the tribes as possible. The prevailing ideology envisioned the transformation of Indians into yeoman farmers. Once they had settled down to the white man's way of farming they would no longer need hunting lands, and additional territory could be opened to white settlement without doing them any real injury. The final step was supposed to be full social and even biological assimilation.

The program failed because it was at variance with the realities of westward expansion and overestimated the willingness of Indians to abandon their traditional culture. White frontiersmen wanted land, not "civilized" Indians. And in the South, where the question of the removal of "the five civilized tribes" became a national issue in the 1820s and 1830s, state governments backed the land-grabbing ambitions of settlers and speculators, and spokesmen for white opinion made it clear that detribalized Indians left behind on farm-sized allotments would be regarded not as candidates for assimilation and citizenship but as free people of color with the same abjectly inferior status as free Negroes. Whatever the federal government and the missionaries might intend for the Indians, the common people of the South and West, who found their spokesman in Andrew Jackson, were determined to remove all Indians, civilized or not, from their midst. When Jackson carried out mass removal of eastern tribes to the trans-Mississippi West in the 1830s, the majority of the philanthropists and missionaries did not object; they rationalized the deportations by arguing that Indians needed a new haven, free from corrupting associations with the wrong kind of whites and the constant pressure of land-hungry settlers, in order to move toward civilization at their own pace.

The story of Indian removal demonstrates the perennial gap that has existed between official rhetoric and ideology and the actual treatment of American Indians. The kind of blatant racism that rationalized the enslavement and segregation of Afro-Americans almost never appeared in official pronouncements, statements by respected political figures, or learned discourses regarding the American Indian. There were some who in the middle decades of the 19th century included the Indians as a prime example of an inferior race allegedly doomed to extinction in the face of competition from biologically superior whites. But the dominant view even then was that Indian extinction, if it occurred, would not be the result of an innate incapacity for civilization but would flow rather from a perverse refusal of the Indian to do what he was perfectly capable of doing—turn himself into a white man. The absence of a strong taboo against intermarriage between whites and Indians (racial blending was in fact positively encouraged by some advocates of the civilization program) provided the strongest evidence that, on an elite level at least, a specifically racial prejudice was not a major factor in American Indian policy. Popular attitudes, especially on the frontier, undoubtedly partook of racial feeling, and in the South particularly there was some transfer of white supremacist ideology from blacks to Indians. But it remains generally true that the Indian was more a victim of cultural than racial bias. From an early period whites have claimed red ancestry with pride and the Indian's physical appearance has often been admired. Whites, of course, have been repulsed by their image of Indian behavior—the savage cruelty of the "wild" redskin and the drunkenness of the reservation Indian. But more often than not these stereotyped defects have been attributed to environment rather than to heredity.

This peculiar situation of racial injustice without ideological racism results in part from the fact that Indians have historically existed in one of two relations with whites: as independent or semi-independent tribesmen who have inspired a combination of fear and respect, or as a conquered people who have ceased to be of any direct concern to most whites. In their first role a motive existed for their subjugation but they did not occasion the contempt that goes with powerlessness. In their second condition, degradation might inspire contempt or pity, but since there was usually no subordinate economic or social role for them to play in white society there was no need for an elaborate ideology of natural inferiority. Because Indians, unlike blacks, were rarely in a position where they represented both an inferior caste and a coerced labor force, they did not inspire the same combination of self-interest, fear, and contempt that underlay the more blatant racism directed at Afro-Americans.

Nineteenth-century Indian policy culminated in the Dawes Act of 1887 which provided for the division of communally held tribal lands into individual allotments. The professed aim, as in all previous federal Indian programs, was the destruction of aboriginal culture and the assimilation of the Indian into American life. The usual blend of white ethnocentrism and humanitarianism led to the usual disaster for the Indians. In fact the period of the allotment program, from 1887 to the 1930s, brought Indian fortunes to their lowest point. Allotment, like removal, resulted in a massive loss of Indian land. Land speculators and mining, timber, and grazing interests not only gained access to the unallotted surplus of tribal land but also succeeded in pressuring many Indians to give up their individual holdings despite safeguards in the law limiting the right of alienation. This was also the era of authoritarian paternalism in government-Indian relations. All-powerful agents and superintendents supplanted the traditional forms of tribal government on the reservations, and the education of Indian children was carried on as much as possible in government boarding schools where a brutal severing of cultural roots was attempted. Because Indians were believed by the cultural evolutionists of the day to be a "backward" people, paternalistic tutelage was deemed necessary as a prelude to acculturation and assimilation. The real injustice to the Indian, and the reason these policies can be considered discriminatory, lay in the fact that Indians were being denied the right to self-determination, the chance to decide for themselves how best to accommodate their ancestral cultures to the demands of the modern world. Hence the congressional legislation of 1924 extending rights of U.S. citizenship to all Indians did not go to the heart of the problem. It was a logical outcome of the policy of forced assimilation and ignored the special kind of collective rights that really mattered to most Indians.

The New Deal era saw a partial reversal of the traditional assimilationist policy. As a result of the Indian Reorganization Act of 1934, the allotment program was stopped and the right to communal ownership of land restored. A modified form of tribal self-government was reinstituted, official encouragement was given to efforts to preserve traditional crafts and customs, and Indians acquired greater potential control over the development of natural resources on tribal lands.

Today the position of Indians in American society is a peculiar and anomalous one. For some purposes they are individual U.S. citizens with all the legal and political rights that this status entails. But those who still live on reservations are also members of communities that enjoy a quasi-autonomous corporate existence outside the Euro-American legal and political structure. The question of what happens when tribal authorities or courts deny individual Indians some of the protections of the Bill of Rights has not yet been completely resolved. Since there is still doubt about what the fundamental rights of Indians really are, it is sometimes difficult to know exactly when they are discriminated against and their rights denied. But from an economic and educational standpoint Indians remain the most disadvantaged of all American minorities. The main source of this persistent poverty and lack of opportunity would seem to lie less in current injustices than in the relative powerlessness of Indians to exert the kind of pressure needed to remedy the legacy of past wrongs. But one form of direct restitution for previous losses seems to be available; in recent years, tribal groups have, with some success, sued in the courts to recover lands ceded in a legally defective way. As in the case of Afro-Americans the plight of the American Indian raises the question as to whether ethnic equality requires not merely even-handedness in the present but also a retroactive compensation—reparations—for injustices that have occurred in the past.

Afro-Americans and the Tyranny of Race

Of all American ethnic groups, Afro-Americans have carried the heaviest burden of prejudice and discrimination. Opinions differ as to how much of this oppression has resulted from an instinctive or deeply rooted color prejudice and how much from the legacy of slavery as an extreme form of social and economic degradation. But most authorities on Afro-American history would agree that both have played a role and that they have reinforced each other at crucial junctures.

Even before they arrived in the New World and began to enslave blacks, many Englishmen had developed a set of negative stereotypes about African character and behavior. Africa itself was usually pictured as the home of the most unmitigated form of "savagery," involving cannibalism, sexual promiscuity, and bizarre forms of pagan ritual. African traits were seen as the direct antithesis of those supposedly distinguishing civilized society, and its savage state had none of the aura of freshness and innocence that sometimes softened the image of the natives of the New World. Furthermore, the African's dark pigmentation conjured up all the associations of blackness with evil and filth that were firmly rooted in European culture and psychology. Finally, as a result of the 16th-century slave trade and the rise of black servitude in Spanish and Portuguese colonies, there was already a popular identification of "blackamoors" with the abject status of slavery. Ethnocentric Englishmen of the early 17th century, who rated other peoples and nationalities in descending order on the basis of how different they were from themselves in appearance, way of life, and apparent achievements, had already placed Africans at the bottom of the hierarchy.

These attitudes predictably led to some discrimination against the earliest Africans arriving in the mainland colonies of North America, most notably the handful brought to Virginia on a Dutch slaver in 1619. Yet the available evidence suggests that discrimination on specifically racial grounds developed gradually over a period of almost a century and closely paralleled the growing dependence on slavery as a system of labor. In the bellwether case of Virginia, the early pattern was one of heavy reliance on white indentured servants who were characteristically treated in a brutal and authoritarian manner until their terms of service were up. Into this labor system a few blacks were introduced before the mid-17th century, and some at least were freed, perhaps because they had fulfilled the labor obligation required of all servants who arrived without specific contracts of indenture. As early as the 1640s, however, some blacks were serving for life, and other signs of discrimination began to appear at the same time. Black women, unlike white female servants, were being used for field work, and a law requiring the arming of servants for defense against Indian attacks excluded blacks. In the 1660s, the enslavement of blacks for life was given legal recognition, and the first law was passed to penalize interracial sex relations. Those blacks who were already freemen first became the target of special legislation in 1670 when they were denied the right to own white servants. But it was not until the early 18th century that free blacks lost the right to vote and hold office in the colony. The emergence of a formalized racial caste system by the 1720s closely paralleled the rise of plantation slavery. The official justification for excluding free blacks from the "great priviledge of a Freeman" in 1723 stressed the danger of free Negroes collaborating with slaves to threaten the security of the newly established forced-labor system.

Blacks could not so easily have been set aside for enslavement and other invidious treatment in Virginia if they had not been readily distinguishable from the rest of the population. Initially the distinction was made on religious grounds: Africans were "heathens" and white colonists were "Christians." Oppression on grounds of deviation from the true faith was a well-established and universally accepted principle in the 17th century. But the progress of Christian conversion among blacks meant that they could no longer be accorded unequal status because of their heathenism. The determination in the 1660s that conversion did not require manumission was part of a gradual shift to an overtly racial rationale for slavery and ultimately for distinctions among free people on the basis of color and ancestry.

But the simple fact of difference—religious or racial—probably is not sufficient to account for the degradation of blacks in colonial America. Blacks were also uniquely vulnerable to such treatment because they had all arrived in the colony aboard slave ships as people utterly devoid of nationality or any personal rights under international law. Unlike free immigrants, they could be legally consigned to any status that the colonial government deemed appropriate. The surprising thing is that it took so long, at least in Virginia, to decide unequivocally that this meant chattel slavery. Furthermore, white colonists had to have some practical motive or incentive to relegate blacks to servitude or caste inferiority. The greatest problem for those seeking to develop the colonies into profitable enterprises was a shortage of labor. Indians had proved unsuitable and, in any case, not enough of them were readily obtainable. White indentured servitude had met the need for a time, but as English economic conditions and population policies changed in the last half of the 17th century, the supply of "sturdy beggars" to be transported to the New World began to dry up. The increasing difficulty of obtaining white servants necessitated shorter terms and better conditions for those already in the New World and thus reduced the convenience and profitability of employing them. Furthermore, white servants eventually became free, and at certain periods, as in the Chesapeake colonies between 1660 and the 1680s, there was little land available for them to settle on as small planters. This situation raised fears among the colonial elite of a landless proletariat threatening the peace of society, fears that seemed realized in 1676 when "the giddy multitude" threw itself with enthusiasm into the insurrection known as Bacon's Rebellion and helped turn a quarrel among the Virginia elite into a virtual civil war. Black slavery was the ultimate solution to this class and labor problem, and the denial of rights also to blacks who were free helped to cement a new solidarity between the upper and lower classes of whites. When the status of freeman was reserved to whites, it tended to elevate the status of those colonists who otherwise had little stake in the established order. It proved relatively easy as time went on to convince lower-class whites that their status gain from the color caste system gave them a real interest in sustaining the dominance of slaveholding planters. Encouragement through legislation of the growing miscegenation phobia was a critical step in the certification of a privileged white caste that transcended class lines. Not only had all the English North American colonies thoroughly institutionalized slavery by the early 18th century, but most of them had also passed stringent laws against interracial marriage. Just as the freedom of whites in the plantation colonies came in the 18th century to depend to some degree upon slavery—for slavery meant that there were no servile and menial roles that whites had to perform—so the equality of whites, or at least the sense of it, came to depend in part on antimiscegenation laws and other caste legislation which stressed the fact that there were no absolute barriers to free association among whites, regardless of putative differences in their class or station. To some extent the fluidity and egalitarianism that was to become such a distinguishing feature of American society by the time of Jackson and Tocqueville was reinforced by racial proscription.

The natural-rights philosophy of the revolutionary era inspired a challenge to slavery which led to gradual emancipation in the North and some questioning of the institution in the South; but those blacks freed by state action or voluntary manumission during this period continued to suffer from most of the disabilities of a pariah class. Liberal southerners like Thomas Jefferson, who sincerely hoped for the ultimate demise of slavery, assumed that the physical differences between races and the prejudices nurtured by slavery would forever prevent whites and black freedmen from living together in peace and equality. Consequently, they coupled their tentative proposals for gradual emancipation with schemes for colonizing the freedmen outside the United States. Such ideas inspired the formation of the American

Society for Colonizing Free People of Color in 1817, an organization manifesting some of the same philanthropic spirit that characterized the Indian civilization movement during the same period. But whereas the Indian civilizationists proclaimed the full incorporation of the red man into American society as their ultimate goal, the colonizationists took it for granted that free blacks were unassimilable because of their "degraded" condition and the "invincible" prejudices of the white population against them.

The abolitionists of the 1830s made the first serious attack on the prevailing practice of racial inequality. Inspired by a perfectionist humanitarianism, they not only called for the immediate abolition of slavery but also denounced the caste barrier in American society. The response of proslavery elements was to articulate the full-blown racist doctrine of inherent black inferiority, an idea that previously had existed only in rudimentary form. The notion that Afro-Americans were natural slaves because they were biologically capable of performing only the most menial and subservient roles was soon buttressed by the science and pseudoscience of the day. A respectable contingent of biologists and ethnologists began to defend as scientific truth the proposition that blacks were created separately from whites and constituted a distinct and permanently inferior species.

In such a climate of opinion the situation of free blacks in both the North and South was bound to deteriorate even further. The basic pattern of exclusion and segregation, often called Jim Crow in the post-Reconstruction South, was implemented in both sections during the ante-bellum period. Free blacks were almost universally denied access to public facilities used by whites or were accommodated separately. Segregation or exclusion was the rule not only in theaters, hotels, taverns, steamboats, and railroad or street cars, but also in churches, prisons, orphanages, and even cemeteries. If blacks received any education at all, they obtained it in separate schools. In the 1830s free blacks were disfranchised in Pennsylvania, North Carolina, and Tennessee, three out of only a handful of states where previously they had voted on the same basis as whites. Some of the states of the Old Northwest, where blacks had never voted or exercised other civil or political rights, attempted in the late ante-bellum period to exclude free blacks entirely by barring their immigration. In the South, laws prohibiting slaves from moving about freely, assembling without white supervision, possessing firearms, or being tried in the same courts and under the same penal code as whites were also applied to free Negroes. On the eve of the Civil War some southern state legislatures were debating proposals designed to expel or enslave all free Negroes in their jurisdictions. The dominant antebellum attitude was the one that Chief Justice Taney, in the *Dred Scott* decision of 1857, attributed to the founding fathers—that Negroes had no rights that white men were bound to respect.

In the South the elaboration of racial caste was related to fears about the future of slavery. Not only were free blacks considered to be potential instigators of slave rebellion, but their very existence as a class in the community undermined the racial rationale for slavery. But discrimination in the North had more complex roots. Although free Negroes constituted only about 1 percent of the total population in the free states in 1860, they tended to be concentrated in a few urban areas where they came into direct economic competition with lower-class whites, especially recent immigrants. But more important than the actual competition with northern workers—an inherently unequal struggle which usually led to the rapid displacement of blacks from jobs coveted by whites—was the fear of future rivalry that might result if southern slaves were freed and migrated northward. Furthermore, the social mobility and disappearance of traditional social and political distinctions that most historians have found characteristic of the Jacksonian era bred status anxieties that could sometimes be assuaged by laying claim in some dramatic way to the automatic prestige that came from the possession of a white skin.

The political struggle that developed after 1846 over the future of slavery in the United States and eventuated in the Civil War was more a contest over the role of slaveholders in the American republic than a disagreement on the basic social position of blacks. But one way to divest southern planters of their power was to take away their slaves, and this was accomplished as an act of "military necessity" during the Civil War. If the destruction of slavery did not signify a national conversion to the principle of racial equality, it did demonstrate at least that a northern majority could recognize higher priorities than the holding of Afro-Americans in abject subjugation. Nationalism was a more important force than racism when the two proved incompatible, as the story of Reconstruction demonstrates. Radical Republicans were influenced to some degree by the abolitionist argument that legalized racial caste was incompatible with American institutions, but a more pressing concern was the fear that the South would return to the Union with the old planter class still in control. Consequently, they attempted by a series of laws and constitutional amendments to create a color-blind legal and political order. Their immediate or practical objective may have been to create a "loyal" (that is, Republican) black electorate in the South, but the long-range effect of their work was to preclude overtly racial tests for national citizenship or for the enjoyment of whatever civil or political rights the courts might be willing to acknowledge as subject to federal protection.

The dominant forces of the white South resisted this program with great energy and ingenuity. As the discriminatory Black Codes passed by southern state legislatures immediately after the war revealed, there was already a well-defined niche waiting for the new freedmen in the southern social structure: they could simply be relegated to the status of ante-bellum free Negroes. Instead of being slaves of individual masters, they would now be servants of the white community in general. When this plan was overruled by the northern radicals, many southerners attempted to reestablish white supremacy by extralegal or illegal methods, intimidating or terrorizing newly enfranchished black voters and using their dominant economic and social position to enforce segregation and discrimination. When Radical Reconstruction was overthrown in the 1870s, the new rulers of the South were able to continue such practices unimpeded by federal intervention. By the 1890s the disappearance of a lingering northern concern about the rights of southern blacks and a series of Supreme Court decisions emasculating the Reconstruction amendments made it possible for southern state legislatures and constitutional conventions to begin giving legal sanction to the pattern of segregation and disfranchisement that had been developing. Between 1890 and 1910 a multitude of Jim Crow laws were passed mandating segregation in virtually all public facilities. This legislation was grounded in the "separate but equal" principle, which meant that a fictive equality in accommodations made segregation nondiscriminatory and hence constitutional—an argument that was formally accepted by the Supreme Court in *Plessy* v. *Ferguson* (1896). Blacks were also deprived of what remained of their suffrage rights by constitutional restrictions on voting that were not explicitly racial but which allowed local registrars to exclude blacks at will from the ballot box. By World War I the southern black electorate had dwindled to almost nothing and segregation in virtually all aspects of social existence from the cradle to the grave was required by law. Segregation could even reach the point of separate phone booths, separate storage facilities for school books used by white and black children, and the use of Jim Crow bibles in courtrooms.

The system of segregation in the South, which would remain virtually intact until the 1950s, was carefully constructed to symbolize the social superiority of the lowest white man to any Negro, no matter how prosperous or accomplished. This suggests that the elaborate system of racial distinctions was designed as much to heal actual or potential rifts among different classes of whites as to hold blacks in subjection. The late 19th- and early 20th-century South was characterized by a crudely exploitative economy with an agricultural system based on a form of tenancy approximating peonage and a nascent industrialization that promised to be competitive with the North only because of the cheapness of its labor. The fact that a large class of poor white farmers and industrial workers coexisted with the mass of black poor constituted both a threat and an opportunity for the dominant elements in southern life. The threat was that an interracial lower class would arise to attack the privileges of the dominant elite of landlords, merchants, and industrialists; for a time the Populist movement of the 1890s seemed to be on the verge of shaping such a coalition. The alternative was to exacerbate racial tensions between poor whites and poor blacks and to buttress the former group's loyalty to the established order by emphasizing their upper-caste position and the psychological rewards of a sense of racial superiority. If this in fact was the strategy of southern elites, it succeeded brilliantly. The implementation of Jim Crow disfranchisement not only reduced blacks to powerlessness and humiliating social inferiority, but also signalled the end of significant political and economic dissent among whites.

The establishment of the new racial order in the South and the new mood of acquiescence in the North were sustained and justified by a barrage of the most virulent racist propaganda that the nation had ever seen. The image of "the Negro as beast" (to quote the title of one of the Negrophobic tracts of the early 1900s) was promulgated in periodicals, books, pamphlets, plays, and motion pictures. Thomas W. Dixon's flagrantly racist *The Clansman* evolved from the bestselling novel of 1905 into a Broadway hit and by 1915 into the most successful of early movies (*The Birth of a Nation*). It brought the image of the vicious and subhuman black, whose lust for white women made him a suitable candidate for lynching, into the center of American consciousness. On a more refined level, scholars invoked Darwinism to legitimize the idea of a "struggle for existence" between the races which the superior whites were destined to win so long as they retained their "racial purity."

The historical development of the 20th century that most affected racial attitudes and practices was the mass migration of blacks from the rural South to the urban North beginning just before World War I. Seeking to escape grinding rural poverty and the rigors of segregation and pulled by the promise of industrial employment, hundreds of thousands of migrants poured into the poorest and most run-down neighborhoods of northern cities. What they found was not precisely what they had left behind but it was still prejudice and discrimination. The northern urban pattern was not segregation by law but the extralegal product of concerted efforts by major institutions and interest groups to exclude blacks from the full advantages of urban and industrial life. Coalitions of white homeowners fought, sometimes with violence, to exclude blacks from their neighborhoods, and overcrowded black ghettos quickly took shape. Trade unions excluded black workers entirely or accepted them only in separate and inferior locals. Trade-union exclusiveness effectively deprived blacks of access to the best industrial jobs, and most were therefore condemned to menial and unskilled occupations. Under the pressure of such circumstances some blacks allowed themselves to be used as strikebreakers by white employers and thereby incited further animosity from white workers. Part of the background of the two great race riots of the World War I era, the East St. Louis, Ill., riot of 1917 and the one that occurred in Chicago two years later, was the familiar story of discrimination by white labor and "scabbing" by blacks. Not until the 1930s with the coming of the New Deal and the efforts of the CIO to organize black workers did Afro-Americans begin to find a secure place in the organized labor force.

Although migration to the North did not bring equality of opportunity, it did provide some sources of strength that helped reduce the powerlessness of the black community. First of all, northern blacks could vote, and by the 1930s white politicians became aware that there were now enough blacks in key industrial states to affect the outcome of elections. Second, blacks had greater opportunities than in the South to organize protest movements and air their grievances. Finally, in times of rapid economic expansion and heightened labor demand, such as existed during both the world wars, they were in a position to make some inroads into skilled and semiskilled occupations previously dominated by whites.

A relative increase in the power and resources available to the black community helps account for the growth of a national commitment to equal rights beginning in the New Deal period. No one pays much attention to the complaints of the powerless, but political leverage and organized pressure compel a response. The effectiveness of black protest between the 1940s and late 1960s also was enhanced by the fact that racist ideologies had been discredited among important elite groups in American society. Well-educated and liberal whites had become increasingly aware of the injustice and irrationality of racial prejudice and discrimination. A combination of black assertiveness and liberalized white attitudes led to a successful assault on the Southern system of segregation in the 1950s and 1960s. But the northern pattern of de facto segregation proved more resistant to change. Although palpable discrimination had certainly been a significant factor in creating this situation, black poverty and a natural tendency toward residential concentration by class and ethnicity may have played a more important role than overtly racist public policies in separating blacks from whites in schools and other local institutions. The intense desire of many whites to preserve an established pattern of white ethnic neighborhoods and schools against black intrusion has proved a powerful and, up to now, insurmountable obstacle to the full integration of northern urban communities. Whether most white resistance to open housing and to court-ordered busing to achieve racial balance in the schools should be viewed as a manifestation of racism or as a legitimate expression of the pluralist character of northern urban life remains a matter of bitter dispute.

The Asian Immigrant as Ultimate Alien — *racial + cultural prejudice*

No category of ethnic Americans has proved capable of arousing, at least temporarily, a more intense and unqualified antipathy than did the Asian immigrants who arrived in California between 1850 and 1908. Neither the paternalism that sometimes took the edge off Negrophobia nor the romanticization that gave the Indian a symbolic dignity were operative in this case. Because he was not white, the Chinese or Japanese newcomer was deemed biologically unassimilable. Because he possessed a culture that differed substantially from the Anglo-American norm, his way of life was denounced as utterly incompatible with American values and behavior. Hence he was simultaneously a victim of the same white-supremacist ethos that condemned blacks and Indians to inferior or marginal status and the object of a particularly virulent strain of nativism—the recurrent hostility to immigrants with cultural backgrounds considered alien to American traditions.

The treatment of recently arrived Asians in California and other western states involved much the same combination of social segregation, economic discrimination, and mob violence that was used to keep blacks "in their place" in the South after Reconstruction. But the main objective of their white enemies was not so much to create a permanent caste system as to exclude Asians entirely from American society. Consequently they not only served for a time as the western surrogate for the blacks of the South but also became the first category of immigrants to be denied free access to the United States.

The Chinese

The first Asians to arrive in substantial numbers were the Chinese who emigrated to California between the 1850s and the 1880s. Welcomed by white entrepreneurs as a source of cheap contract labor for mining, railroad construction, and manufacturing, they encountered bitter hostility from white workers and small businessmen who viewed them as actual or potential competitors. The substantive complaint of these groups was that Asians were semislaves who accepted wages and working conditions which no white man would tolerate and that they consequently aided the land, railroad, and mining barons in their efforts to monopolize the sources of western wealth that once had seemed open to all enterprising migrants from the East and Europe. But such appeals to tangible white interests were heavily overlaid and sometimes even obscured by racist assaults on the Chinese as opium smokers, carriers of exotic oriental diseases, and devotees of sexual practices that threatened the health and purity of the white community. The image of the Chinese as drug-addicted, sexually depraved barbarians provoked a western equivalent of the miscegenation phobia directed toward Afro-Americans in other sections and resulted in similar forms of mob action against alleged offenders.

After the Civil War, anti-Chinese sentiment emerged as a decisive force in California politics. The Democrats used it first as a device to regain their ante-bellum dominance, but in the late 1870s a combination of economic distress and popular dissatisfaction at Democratic accommodation with employers of Chinese labor provoked a strong third-party movement devoted to repression of the Chinese for the benefit of white labor. The Workingman's party of California, led by the Irish immigrant Dennis Kearney, was strongly represented at the state constitutional convention of 1878 and took the lead in enacting clauses prohibiting the employment of Chinese labor and giving local authorities carte blanche to "abate" the "Chinese menace" in any way they saw fit. Such actions were in fact mainly symbolic, for they flagrantly violated the U.S. Constitution and were overturned in federal courts. But the long-simmering California agitation for an end to all Chinese immigration bore fruit in 1882 when the Chinese Exclusion Act was passed by the U.S. Congress. This legislation reflected the fact that Sinophobia was not limited to California or the western states but had by now become part of the larger American pattern of ethnic prejudice. On a national level, as in California, spokesmen for white labor led the agitation for the first federal immigration law discriminating against a specific nationality, but it is indicative of the friendless situation of the Chinese that there was little opposition to the policy from other groups.

Hostility to the Chinese did not end with the closing of the gates but actually peaked in the mid-1880s when there was an epidemic of forced expulsions of entire Chinese communities from mining and lumbering towns all over the Far West. But the subsequent concentration of the remaining Chinese in a few virtually self-sufficient enclaves, most notably San Francisco's Chinatown, and in a few noncompetitive enterprises such as laundries and Chinese restaurants eventually resulted in a decline of active white antagonism. In the 20th century there has been a steady decrease of anti-Chinese prejudice due to such factors as the social and economic success of Sino-Americans, the projection of a more favorable image of their communal and cultural life, and—despite the notable ups and downs associated with the Communist assumption of power in mainland China and the Korean War—a general accretion of respectful attitudes toward China itself.

The Japanese

Although Chinese immigration was legally ended in 1882, the door was still open to other Asians, and substantial numbers of Japanese began to arrive in California during the 1890s. Most established themselves as farm workers and then as small independent farmers, successfully employing Japanese methods of intensive agriculture. As in the case of the Chinese, white agitation for discrimination and exclusion was quick to develop. The new Asian immigrants were excoriated as the vanguard of a "yellow peril"—a tide of inferior humanity supposedly rolling out of the East and threatening to engulf the United States. Prominent in the anti-Japanese campaign were labor groups and organizations of white farmers reacting to competition from the more efficient Japanese cultivators. In 1906 the San Francisco School Board responded to the growing clamor by ordering the segregation of white and Asian children. But the emergence of Japan as a major world power at the beginning of the century made open discrimination against its nationals more difficult than the earlier mistreatment of the Chinese, whose home government had been weak and subservient to Western interests. When the imperial government issued a formal protest against school segregation in San Francisco, President Theodore Roosevelt intervened in the controversy: in 1907 and 1908 he negotiated a withdrawal of the offending ordinance in return for a "gentlemen's agreement" from Japan to terminate emigration to the United States. But the assault on the rights of Japanese immigrants continued in California, culminating in 1913 in a law denying the right of land ownership to "aliens ineligible for citizenship" which in effect singled out the Japanese and attempted to destroy their competitive position in California agriculture. (Japanese were not considered potential citizens because the original U.S. naturalization law limiting eligibility to "free white persons" had never been amended to include Asians.)

Although association with a powerful Japanese nation provided some limited protection to Japanese-Americans in the early 20th century, the putative Japanese nationality of their descendants proved disastrous during World War II. In the most flagrant act of discrimination against any immigrant group in American history, the federal government in 1942 ordered the forced removal and internment of the entire

Japanese population of the Pacific Coast, including native-born citizens of the United States. Wartime hysteria and an urge for symbolic revenge against the perpetrators of Pearl Harbor provide only part of the explanation for this unprecedented denial of civil rights. Without the century-long tradition of anti-Asian prejudice in the United States—a bias that characteristically took the form of treating Asian immigrants as the most unwelcome and unassimilable of "aliens" —such a drastic act of repression would probably have been unthinkable.

Since the end of the war there has been a dramatic decline in prejudice and discrimination against Japanese and other Asians. Special restrictions on Asian immigration have been lifted, and the prospects for upward mobility and assimilation have markedly improved for individuals of Asian descent. As far as the Japanese were concerned, this change was related to such factors as the new status of Japan as an ally of the United States, white guilt over wartime excesses, the greater geographic dispersal of the Japanese population after release from internment, and certain characteristics of Japanese-American culture that have promoted individual and collective achievement. It may be premature to claim that racial prejudice against Asians has disappeared, but the trend appears to be in the direction of according to Americans of various Asian ancestries a status roughly equivalent to that of white "ethnics." If this tendency continues, it will provide strong evidence that racism is a situational and historically determined phenomenon and not the result of some innate "consciousness of kind."

Hispanic Americans

Like the Asian minorities, Spanish-speaking Americans have been the victims of a combination of ethnocultural and racial prejudice. The social effects of such attitudes, together with the growing size of the Spanish-speaking population, have made this minority among the most conspicuous in contemporary America. Actually, it is misleading to talk about a single Hispanic group, for Mexicans, Puerto Ricans, and Cubans differ in a number of significant ways, and there are a good many other small groups from Spanish-speaking backgrounds. Their historical experiences are sufficiently dissimilar to preclude any uniform conclusions about the sources and effects of the prejudices they have encountered in American life. By and large they were incorporated into the population of the United States at different times and through different processes. Historically they have inhabited widely removed areas of the country. Their racial make-up is different; each has established a distinctive relationship with its cultural homeland; and the position each occupies in American society accords them differential ability to protect themselves against discrimination.

The Mexicans

One segment of the Mexican-American community became part of the United States through conquest in the 19th century, another through immigration, largely in the 20th century. In the 1840s and 1850s the annexation of Texas, the war with Mexico, and the Gadsden Purchase added thousands of Spanish-speaking residents to the population of the United States. Placed in the position of a conquered people, they confronted strong Anglo-American antipathies. In Texas, especially, they bore the "burden of the Alamo," the stigma of a despised alien enemy. Their concentration in established communities, their fidelity to the Roman Catholic Church, and the proximity of Mexico itself ensured that the Mexican-American population of the new Southwest maintained a cultural insularity that would continue to mark it as foreign in the eyes of ethnocentric Anglo-Americans. In the states of California and Texas as well as in the territories of Colorado, New Mexico, and Arizona, Mexicans shared the status of indigens with Indians, and like the Indians they possessed a commodity—land—that Anglo-Americans coveted. To race-conscious 19th-century Americans, particularly to the southerners who came to inhabit Texas, their mixed racial ancestry gave license for abuse. Where they remained local majorities, numbers afforded a certain protection against social slights and economic exploitation. To penetrate the most populous Spanish-speaking communities of Arizona and New Mexico, Anglo-Americans frequently had to amalgamate with the Spanish elites. But Anglo-American migration in pursuit of the profits of mining, ranching, and railroading made it inevitable that the Mexicans of the Southwest would eventually become statewide or territorial minorities. Without political influence that extended much beyond their own immediate communities, Mexican-Americans became relatively powerless to repel predatory raids upon their land and assaults on their cultural inheritance. Anglo-American land commissions gradually extinguished traditional property titles, and legislatures made English the official language of government in the cause of Americanization. In Texas, many fundamental protections of the law were stripped from Mexican-Americans as from blacks by the institution of white primary elections at the turn of the century.

Immigrants from Mexico began to supplement the native-born Spanish-speaking population of the southwestern United States in the mid-19th century. Mexican miners participated in the gold rush to California during the 1840s and railroad workers passed over the international boundary in pursuit of employment as the lines of northern Mexico reached completion. In Arizona and New Mexico the newcomers reinforced the local dominance of established Spanish-American communities. But in Texas and California they swelled the ranks of a propertyless laboring class analogous to the Chinese of the Far West or to the black population of the post–Civil War South and thus invited exploitation by employers or landlords and the antipathy of native white workers.

Political disruptions associated with the Mexican Revolution and a variety of economic pressures greatly accelerated the pace of Mexican immigration to the United States in the 20th century. An open border enabled Mexican laborers to respond to employment opportunities on either side. The transient nature of some elements of the Mexican minority in the United States frequently provided Anglo-American public officials with arguments for withholding public education, welfare benefits, and political recognition from the Spanish-speaking community altogether.

Despite the clamor about the racial decay of the United States which peaked during the early 1920s, Mexicans were specifically excluded from the immigration quotas of 1921 and 1924 at the behest of southwestern employers. But by establishing the principle that only Mexicans unlikely to become a public charge were welcome to enter the United States, the national origins acts gave government officials a powerful administrative tool for adjusting the supply of immigrants to domestic economic demand. During the Great Depression this regulation was sometimes enforced with brutal efficiency. Mexican laborers were repeatedly routed from their jobs in favor of "white" Americans, and the unemployed aliens were conveyed south of the border. Substantial numbers of bona fide U.S. citizens were rounded up and threatened with expulsion because they "looked" Mexican. The Los Angeles "Zoot Suit" riots which followed during the 1940s, pitting "Anglo" servicemen against Mexican-American youth, confirmed with chilling clarity the exposure of the Hispanic community to the possibility of racial aggression and discrimination.

During the last quarter-century, Mexican-Americans have become a highly visible and somewhat segregated minority. Although economic developments have transformed them from a regional to a national minority and from a largely rural population to an increasingly urban one, they remain heavily concentrated in the southwestern United States. Proximity to the Mexican border and international family ties have combined with regional concentration to encourage the preservation of a vital ethnic culture. Concentration and cultural vitality have stimulated ethnocultural bias, but they have also helped the Mexican-American community of the Southwest to organize politically in the post–Civil Rights era to protect itself from public or private discrimination.

The Immigration Act of 1965 produced a new source of anti-Mexican hostility in the United States. By establishing immigration quotas for hemispheric neighbors, the new regulations produced a much larger number of illegal, or undocumented, immigrants, many of them Mexican workers who continued to exercise their traditional liberty of crossing the border unofficially in pursuit of employment. The American economic recession of the 1970s transformed them into an emotionally charged political issue. "Illegals" were accused of stimulating the unemployment of U.S. citizens and of depressing workers' wages. Other Americans express the fear that hordes of racially inferior "brown" Mexicans will undermine traditional American cultural values. Their undocumented status compounds the difficulties that Mexicans may face in the United States. By choice and circumstance, "illegals" are among the most unprotected and disadvantaged classes in the United States. Fearful of detection and expulsion, they are largely without the protection of the laws, isolated from agencies of public welfare, and in some ways at the mercy of employers. Although Mexican-American citizens are sometimes among the most vocal critics of the "illegals," the issue has embittered many Anglos against the Mexican-American community generally. Chicano political activists argue that this is evidence that Spanish-speaking minorities continue to face a malicious strain of racial prejudice in American society.

The Puerto Ricans

Puerto Ricans, in contrast, have held legal status as immigrants to the continental United States since 1898, when

Puerto Rico became a U.S. possession. New facilities for trans-Caribbean travel at the conclusion of World War II encouraged Puerto Ricans to escape chronic overpopulation and underemployment and seek improved economic opportunities on the mainland. This quest took them mostly to major industrial metropolitan areas, particularly New York City and Chicago. Arriving with few marketable skills or material resources, most immigrants found employment as low-paid wage laborers in manufacturing and the service industries. A high rate of fertility among this population inhibited family saving and social mobility, and the language barrier interfered with education and occupational advancement. Economic conditions condemned most Puerto Ricans to residence in decaying inner-city environments. On the whole, the Puerto Rican minority has found it even more difficult than blacks to escape the grip of urban poverty.

Puerto Ricans' ethnic identity in the United States is a compound of class, cultural, and racial distinctiveness. To some extent the ethnic group displays the characteristics of the inner-city poor generally. But their Hispanic culture makes them stand out from other working-class elements. Residential concentration and the continued accretion of newcomers from Puerto Rico reinforce cultural uniqueness in the urban environment. Although the Puerto Rican population represents many degrees of racial admixture as evidenced in a wide variety of physical types, non-Hispanic Americans have tended to lump its members together as part of a "brown" race. This classification has inhibited the amalgamation of Puerto Ricans with either blacks or whites and has consequently prevented dilution of the ethnic group's other distinguishing features.

Because of their multiple sources of group identity, Puerto Ricans have encountered a complex assortment of suspicions and prejudices in the mainland United States. Populated by a singularly poverty-stricken social class, Puerto Rican communities often strike more fortunate Americans as burdensome pockets of urban decay, welfare expense, and street crime, as well as new sources of unwelcome cultural or linguistic diversity. Working-class ethnic groups sometimes regard them as economic interlopers, stimulating unemployment and depressing wages. Detractors also charge that the social immobility that has locked much of the Puerto Rican minority into urban barrios is encouraged by voluntary clannishness. Puerto Ricans themselves frequently insist that their economic opportunities have been hampered by a lack of education fostered by an ethnocentric language barrier. But efforts to promote bilingualism in the schools often run athwart the potent argument that it represents a dysfunctional resistance to acculturation which compounds existing economic disabilities. Because of the popular tendency to identify Puerto Ricans as nonwhites, they are open to insinuations that poverty and cultural insularity are products of innate racial proclivities and that fuller integration into American society is unlikely. Whether individual Puerto Ricans encounter racial prejudice depends in part upon personal physical features. But because the ethnic group as a whole is regarded as homogeneous, individuals may find themselves held responsible for the actions or characteristics of any other member of the minority: Puerto Rican community leaders argue that law enforcement officers often harass an entire population for the transgressions of a few.

Both poverty and prejudice have made it difficult for Puerto Ricans to get ahead in the United States. Like other ghetto dwellers, they experience the high economic costs of inner-city living which impede mobility. Racial and cultural prejudices interfere with Puerto Ricans' ability to join with other urban and working-class minorities in the pursuit of common interests. Unlike Mexican-Americans, Puerto Ricans generally have not been able to make effective use of residential concentration to promote group goals or provide political protections for civil rights. As metropolitan rather than statewide or regional minorities, Puerto Ricans' political influence has been almost entirely local, making the mobilization of state and national government on their behalf more difficult.

The Cubans

Cubans constitute the smallest of the three major Spanish-speaking ethnic minorities in the United States and are among the most recent arrivals. Few Cubans migrated to the United States before the 1959 revolution. The large numbers who arrived thereafter moved chiefly for political reasons. Admitted to the United States as refugees, the vast majority of immigrants were voluntary exiles from Castro's revolution. The Cuban immigration also differs from the Mexican and Puerto Rican in other important respects. Flight took Cubans to the closest point on the mainland, Miami, Fla., where for the most part they have remained, in regional isolation. This extreme concentration, together with a strong entrepreneurial ethic among the Cuban population, has produced considerable material prosperity. To a great extent, whatever prejudice the Cuban minority of south Florida has encountered has been much like that aimed at Japanese or Jewish Americans, motivated more by economic jealousy than by disrespect. The economic and political strength produced by concentration, however, has given Cuban Americans powerful weapons for warding off the potential social consequences of prejudice.

Cuban Americans have been spared much of the racial bias directed at Mexicans and Puerto Ricans largely because blacks and other dark-skinned racial mixtures were underrepresented in the movement to the mainland. Nonetheless, economic self-sufficiency, political clout, and the superpatriotism popularly associated with the Cubans' intense anti-Communism have been at least as important as white skin in maintaining the group's freedom from the more serious expressions of prejudice and acts of discrimination faced by other Hispanics. In fact, the Cuban experience seems to demonstrate the extent to which the model of assimilation followed by many European ethnic groups remains operative and the way in which Spanish-speaking groups may be able to overcome ethnocultural and class biases without surrendering a distinctive cultural identity and community residential patterns.

Although each of the Spanish-speaking ethnic groups in the United States encounters different degrees of prejudice in American society, the fundamental sources of ethnic antipathy are similar. In the immediate future it is unlikely that prejudice against the Spanish-speaking will disappear. Despite interethnic marriages, socioeconomic advancement, and residential mobility, the size of culturally distinctive Hispanic communities continues to grow. The number of Spanish-speaking newcomers so far exceeds the numbers assimilating into the larger society that these ethnic groups are sometimes called "eternal first-generation" immigrants, for they have a constantly reinforced ethnocultural identity. Economic differences and barrio residential characteristics reinforce ethnic distinctiveness and provide outsiders with reasons or excuses for fear and disdain. Native prejudice helps sustain these conditions. Economic disabilities, in particular, bring criticism and encourage exploitation.

The relative freedom of the U.S. Cuban population from ethnic prejudice suggests that socioeconomic advancement may eventually emancipate the other Hispanic minorities from bias and exploitation. The success of the Mexican and Puerto Rican minorities depends to some extent upon their ability to take advantage of residential concentration to promote economic self-help and acquire political leverage.

European Immigrants and Anglo-American Nativism

Before the English colonizers of North America had completed their assessment of blacks and Indians or begun to react to Asians or Hispanics, newcomers from Europe were challenging the ethnic homogeneity of white society itself. First as a trickle, then as a flood, the Atlantic migration introduced millions to the New World between the 17th and mid-20th centuries and deposited ethnic communities representing virtually every European nationality or would-be nationality. During times of peace, prosperity, and popular self-assurance, the United States proved remarkably receptive to this growing ethnic diversity. But in periods of crisis, colonial-stock Americans frequently singled out ethnic groups as sources of social disharmony and communal weakness. From an early date, Anglo-Americans regarded political and religious affinities as touchstones of the immigrants' potential loyalty and capacity for assimilation. Successive generations of the American-born majority—a fluid category variously labeling itself as Anglo-American, Anglo-Saxon, or Old Stock—in turn identified Roman Catholicism, Judaism, and all varieties of unrepublican "radicalism" as the principal threats to national unity and progress. Until the 20th century, American society accepted immigrants without impediment, yet popular ethnocentrism demanded that newcomers conform to the social myths, values, and traditions of old-stock Americans. The idea that American identity was accessible only to particular ethnic groups usually remained dormant. But in times of the most acute social or intellectual crisis, elements of the native majority proved themselves willing and able to redefine nationality in purely ethnic terms to keep immigrants and their children from centers of power and influence in American life and thus to maintain their own social dominance.

Colonial and Early National Periods

The English settlers of 17th-century North America brought with them strong nationalist biases that affected their reception of subsequent European migrants. In the colonies, the anti-Catholic animus that was part of the contemporary Englishman's national identity vented itself not only on those who arrived under the banners of imperial rivals France and Spain but also on some of the Scots and Irish who composed part of the colonial trade in indentured servants. Roman Catholicism impressed Anglo-American colonists as a source of immorality and political unreliability; few English settlements in the New World failed to protect themselves from subversion by erecting impediments to Catholic immigration. The conditions and motives of colonization reinforced the initial disposition of Anglo-Americans to view ethnic differences in nationalistic and cultural terms. Perched on the edge of a wilderness 3,000 miles from the homeland, yet unshakably committed to remaining an identifiably English people, the colonists clung tenaciously to traditional values and prejudices. The expressly religious foundations of several colonies reinforced sectarian bigotries transported from Europe. In New England the covenantal form of community organization was utterly antithetical to cultural pluralism of any sort.

Colonial Anglo-Americans employed preponderance in numbers and an initial monopoly of political power to insist upon the acculturation of the other Europeans who came to settle among them, thrusting the most recalcitrant nonconformists to the geographical fringes of society. During the 65 years preceding the American Revolution successive waves of Scotch-Irish and German arrivals settled in disproportionate numbers along a great western arc beyond the centers of English population. There they found themselves able to retain considerable cultural distinctiveness free from Anglo-American interference. Thus, during the colonial period of American history, physical space effectively inhibited interethnic tension or at least impeded active discrimination against disapproved minorities.

Proscriptions placed by the first colonists upon the civil rights of Catholic settlers were weakened in the early 18th century in consequence of the increase of sectarian diversity among Protestants themselves. Foreign-born colonists responded so energetically to the relaxation of religious tests in politics that many traditionalists feared the eclipse of English governance and cultural predominance. Only half in jest, Benjamin Franklin suggested that future generations of Pennsylvanians school themselves in the German language lest they become strangers in their native land. In several colonies ethnocultural friction intruded into politics. Political contention between backcountry and seacoast in the Southern colonies during the immediate prerevolutionary period frequently had an ethnic dimension. Although events leading to the Revolution itself temporarily reinvigorated anti-Catholic prejudices, the principal effect of the struggle for colonial home rule was to persuade Anglo-Americans of the fundamental loyalty of major white ethnic minorities.

During the early years of the American republic a new conviction that political culture was bound up with emerging nationalism supplanted some of the traditional distinctions that Americans had made between white ethnic groups. As Anglo-Americans came to think of themselves as a unique people, not even new arrivals from England were wholly exempt from suspicion. European challenges to the sovereignty of the fledgling United States between 1790 and 1815 provoked a temporary but widespread xenophobia exceeding the ethnocultural suspicions of the colonial era. Increasingly, Americans regarded deviations from their Protestant, bourgeois, and individualistic culture as symptomatic of antirepublican tendencies. In particular, old-stock Americans associated Roman Catholicism with monarchist leanings.

Because popular thought increasingly identified political ideology with ethnicity, public debate over U.S. foreign relations and domestic party conflict were breeding grounds for interethnic tension. Jeffersonians, despite their advertisement of the United States as a refuge for Europe's oppressed, feared that British and German immigrants might infect U.S. institutions with monarchical tendencies. Their rivals, the Federalists, expressed even greater concern at the prospect that newcomers from France and Ireland would bear the dangerous enthusiasms of the French Revolution. During the Federalist ascendancy of the 1790s, naturalization law was deliberately employed to discourage the immigration of either the Celtic Irish or the French and to keep the votes of the foreign-born out of Republican tallies. By extending the period of probationary residence for citizenship applicants from 5 to 14 years in 1798, Congress intended to protect the republic from alien subversives already on the soil. The principal targets were Irish Americans, whom Anglo-American conservatives regarded as having "red republican" leanings. Only a relative liberalization of the official treatment of immigrants accompanied the political "revolution" of 1800 which brought Thomas Jefferson to the presidency. The Democratic-Republicans, much like the Federalists, demanded total acculturation of immigrants as proof of loyalty and were prepared to manipulate naturalization laws to exclude those foreigners they found dangerous or unattractive. Although they repealed the Naturalization Act of 1798, the Democratic-Republicans responded to the hostility toward England that grew during the early years of the 19th century by placing mildly punitive conditions upon the residence of British aliens. In 1813 Congress stipulated that no British alien who had not declared an intention to become a U.S. citizen before the onset of the War of 1812 could be naturalized, a provision repealed after the war ended. Once ethnicity became entangled with American politics, simple ethnocultural differences between the native- and foreign-born lost some of their earlier salience. The Anglo-American majority increasingly focused its concern on the few immigrant groups that seemed to have either the size or the foreign connections to threaten seriously the republican system of government or the security of the nation. Late 18th- and early 19th-century ethnic antipathy, therefore, was directed primarily at French, Irish, and, to some extent, English immigrants. Perceived ideological affinities had replaced gross cultural differences as the primary stimulants of prejudice.

The Ante-Bellum Years

Ethnicity remained a popular shorthand indication of political allegiance until the Civil War. Ante-bellum political adversaries proved capable of cynically manipulating anti-immigrant feeling to serve their immediate interests. Democrats denounced Illuminism, Free Masonry, and monarchism as immigrant-borne threats to the ideology of republican simplicity. Refugee forty-eighters from the German principalities, on the other hand, impressed Whigs as anarchists and moral libertines. The Irish, who began arriving in the United States in larger numbers during the 1830s, could be regarded as either the Pope's reactionary minions or as dangerous republican radicals and were alternately castigated by both Whig and Democratic politicians. It was the Whig party, however, which denounced most volubly the connection between Roman Catholicism and Old World despotism, and in time the Democrats absorbed the larger number of naturalized citizens.

Anti-Catholicism acquired a new and more highly charged meaning during the decades before the Civil War, a period when Americans were struggling to create a distinctive national identity shorn of the taints of Europe. For a people trying to discover who they were and what gave them national unity, identification of a historical enemy proved enormously useful. Accused by both native and foreign critics of excessive individualism and contentiousness, ante-bellum Americans lashed out at tangible evidence of clannishness and separatism. A popular theme in American political rhetoric during the 1820s and 1830s was opposition to secret, "subversive" organizations. Exclusivity of all kinds was denounced as antithetical to democratic notions of public openness and equality. Inevitably, ethnic fellowships—and especially the Roman Catholic Church—became targets for politicians who proclaimed them sources of disharmony in American life. The immigrants' efforts to ease the pain of transplantation and reinforce a distinctive cultural identity through mutual-aid societies and social clubs made them especially vulnerable to such charges.

The growth of the idea that the United States was destined to perform a regenerative world mission offered another kind of response to the midcentury crisis of national identity. Ante-bellum Anglo-Americans eagerly sponsored Protestant evangelical missions as part of a national crusade to bring enlightenment to the heathen and the unregenerate. Immigrant Catholics threatened this whole concept of national unification and self-justification because of their reluctance to support such popular evangelical reforms as temperance and strict sabbatarianism. Aggressive Protestant agencies like the American Home Missionary Society and the Society for the Diffusion of Christian Knowledge devoted considerable effort to counteracting what evangelistic Protestants regarded as the deleterious effects of Romanism upon the republic. Native-born Protestants, convinced that the public schools were the proper instrument for instilling national values in youth, fiercely resisted immigrants' efforts to introduce sectarian teachings into state-supported education and attacked the creation of alternative parochial institutions of learning. The burning of the Charlestown, Mass., convent school by an enraged Protestant mob in 1834 illustrates the strength of this sentiment in some quarters.

When perfectionist reform faltered, opportunistic politicians capitalized on popular demands for a ritual national housecleaning by adopting the cause of naturalization reform. During the 1830s and 1840s Whig demagogues—and in some locales Democrats—took to the stump to persuade native-born voters that their ballots were being diluted by numbers of ill-educated and tractable foreigners, fresh off the boat, who had been brought before a partisan judge, summarily naturalized, and then marched to the polls. The proposed remedy to such corruption was an extension of the residency requirement for prospective citizens to as long as 21 years. The argument that such reforms would do much to purify U.S. politics possessed such popular appeal that when the major parties were slow to translate rhetoric into legislation, political splinter groups eagerly seized upon the program as a source of easy access to the electorate. In 1836 Samuel F. B. Morse, later to invent the telegraph, ran strongly for mayor of New York City on a pledge of naturalization reform as the candidate of the newly founded Native Democratic Association. In 1845 several of these nativist associations from the eastern states merged in Philadelphia to form a national Native American party. During the early 1850s Know-Nothings captured the governorship of Massachusetts, gained positions of influence in a handful of state legislatures, and filled a number of seats in the U.S. Congress. Recognizing the popularity of the theme of naturalization reform, the newly organized Republican party adopted the issue in some states as part of its initial campaign program. After being dropped by the Republicans because of the offense it gave to some ethnic groups which the party wished to attract, naturalization reform reemerged as part of efforts lasting through the election of 1860 to create a conservative and intersectional Unionist party that could sidestep the divisive slavery issue.

During the 1840s and 1850s the number of newcomers to the United States from Germany and Ireland grew at an unprecedented rate and tangible conflicts of interest between native- and foreign-born Americans became more acute, thus reinforcing political nativism. In northeastern seaboard cities, where the bulk of the famine-stricken Irish initially concentrated, competition between the native-born and immigrants for employment and housing exacerbated hostility to foreigners. Immigration was no longer exclusively the concern of society's moral and cultural leadership; ethnic prejudice also made considerable headway among the native-born laboring classes. The emergence of distinctive ethnic neighborhoods across the urban landscape produced cultural friction which far exceeded that of the colonial period. Fingers of Irish settlement along expanding railroad and canal routes and burgeoning German farm communities in the Northwest also produced unprecedented cultural cleavages in the rural United States. The clash of folkways, mores, and religions sometimes led only to the dissemination of humorously derisive ethnic stereotypes in American popular culture—like the brew-saturated, pot-bellied German plowman. But it also created enduring ethnic hostility toward the reputedly un-American "bog" Irish.

Interethnic competition, both material and ideological, produced considerable physical violence during the decades around mid-century. Rivalry between Anglo-American and immigrant fire companies, militia units, and street gangs resulted in murderous affrays in the streets of Baltimore, New York, and Boston. The so-called Bible Riots, which incinerated whole blocks of Philadelphia during the spring and summer of 1844, grew out of a complex of interethnic economic, political, and religious competition and criminal provocations that pitted Irish Catholics against Protestant Orangemen and Anglo-Americans. Inhabitants of Washington, D.C., came to expect an outbreak of ethnic violence every election day. The Louisville election-day riot of 1855 was so sanguinary that it became known as Bloody Monday.

Inevitably, some ante-bellum Anglo-Americans were persuaded that the failure of immigrants to be completely absorbed into American society reflected an innate inability to acculturate. As early as the 1830s there were fitful efforts to tie American national character to ethnic inheritance. The scientific theory of the plural origins of the "types of mankind," popular among some southern defenders of racial slavery, could also be extended to explain enduring "racial" differences among white Americans. During the 1840s and 1850s some observers of the nation's increasingly polyglot population worked out intricate associations between the real or imagined physical peculiarities of white ethnic stocks and their cultural, religious, and political proclivities. Parlor pseudosciences like phrenology and physiognomy groomed an entire generation of middle-class Americans to accept the idea that the smallest differences in physical form revealed important distinctions in intelligence and character.

Although the champions of naturalization reform and militant Protestantism might have found support in a racialist explanation of ethnic differences, popular theories about the degraded Celts and the noble Saxons made surprisingly little headway among the principal nativist organizations of the mid-19th century. Political nativists like the Know-Nothings remained committed to a cultural interpretation of nationality in which education and acculturation rather than birth qualified individuals for U.S. citizenship. Racialist Anglo-Saxonism surfaced primarily in the form of unflattering ethnic stereotypes—especially of the Irish—that entered into everyday American language. Undoubtedly the persistence of such images in popular culture fueled native bias against immigrants. But institutionalized "racial" discrimination against mid-century ethnic groups could not be rigorously sustained in the face of the reality that it was almost impossible to differentiate physically between Anglo-Americans and the foreign-born. The popular fiction that the peoples of Western Europe owed their origins to separate sources suffered during the Civil War years when military medical examiners had the opportunity to compare the physical characteristics of tens of thousands of citizen-soldiers. In fact, the patriotism and valorous military service of immigrants from a variety of European backgrounds during the conflict seemed proof that the newcomers were fully capable of absorbing American values and loyalties.

The Late 19th Century

Accelerating urbanization, industrialization, and changing patterns of social mobility combined during the three decades following the Civil War to give many Americans a deep sense of dislocation and anomie. Because of their concentration in urban areas and characteristic status as industrial workers, European immigrants effectively symbolized these developments and became natural targets for Americans threatened and disoriented by change. In a sense, ethnic groups became distinguished less by their particular cultural heritages than by the social and economic position they occupied in American society. Although this development eased prejudice against the German and Irish immigrants of the early 19th century (who had begun to work their way into the middle class), it made acculturation more difficult for subsequent waves of newcomers.

The rebounding economy of the immediate post–Civil War years stimulated the receptivity of American employers to accelerated European immigration. A number of states actually responded to businessmen's lobbies by passing contract-labor laws that facilitated the recruitment of workers abroad. Official encouragement of immigration sometimes extended to bounty arrangements and tax exemptions for new arrivals. Because this sanguine view of immigration possessed a fundamentally economic basis, it was repeatedly threatened and finally killed by fluctuating business conditions. The depressions of the middle 1870s, 1880s, and 1890s dampened the enthusiasm for immigration among industrialists. During these episodes of national distress, immigrants appeared a burden on already oversaturated labor markets. Second thoughts about the wisdom of unrestricted European immigration gained impetus when businessmen faced the specter of industrial strikes and labor radicalism fueled by layoffs and wage reductions.

Economic pressures also influenced the character of interethnic relations within the American working class itself during the final quarter of the 19th century. During the depression of the mid-1870s workers' organizations in several states pressured legislators to rescind the contract-labor laws of the 1860s and eliminate other inducements for immigrants. Between 1871 and 1875 violence wracked the coalfields of western Pennsylvania when Anglo-American and Irish miners fought the introduction of poorly paid Italian and eastern European immigrants into the mines. In the midst of another recession a decade later, emergent labor unions petitioned for a federal immigrant head tax to reduce the flow of new entrants to the U.S. labor pool and lobbied with individual states for legal bars to the employment of the foreign-born on public-works projects. Organized labor especially resented the use of immigrants as strikebreakers and denounced them as ignorant tools of grasping pluto-crats.

While competition for employment was a powerful stimulant of interethnic hostility among working-class Americans, even more intense anti-immigrant prejudices developed among members of a U.S.-born middle class largely insulated from direct contact with foreigners. During the late 19th century these genteel nativists increasingly perceived untrammeled immigration as a multifaceted threat to their traditional status and opportunities. Immigrants conveniently symbolized the problems posed by an expanding urban industrial proletariat. In immigrant ghettos middle-class Americans discerned a breeding ground for social disorder and crime. "Incurable" European poverty could thus be held responsible for the continuing deterioration of the nation's urban cores. The persistence of an economic subclass apparently trapped in poverty appeared to threaten the middle-class ideal of a mobile, homogeneous population. As the national self-confidence and self-congratulation that characterized the first years after the Civil War drained away, concern about political subversion and foreign radicalism reemerged. Labor-management strife during the Gilded Age stimulated fears of socialism, Communism, and other "European" radicalisms. Such movements not only seemed culturally alien, but also appeared to owe their existence to a growing industrial proletariat composed mainly of recent foreign arrivals. It was easy to attribute the persistence of an urban lower class to the inability of immigrants to grasp the ethic of industry, frugality, and sobriety that reputedly led to upward mobility. Ironically, at the same time that the foreign-born were denounced as fomenters of labor unrest, they were also often perceived by those in the middle ranks of society as the tools of grasping capitalists, employed to shatter a free labor market and the American dream of social mobility. Bowing to these sorts of fears, Republican conventions in Pennsylvania and Ohio endorsed federal immigration restriction in 1887.

Throughout the last quarter of the 19th century anti-Catholicism proved a useful vehicle for expressing class and ethnic insecurity. Immigrant Catholicism became a kind of identifying tag attached to the urban poor and a symbol of the social problems commonly associated with them. This identification was effectively developed by Josiah Strong in his contribution to the literature of Anglo-American nationalism, *Our Country*, published in 1885. Resurgent anti-Catholicism became endemic among rural and small-town native-born Americans. This sentiment represented their alienation from urban, industrial, cosmopolitan society and was the basis of the nativistic American Protective Association founded in Clinton, Iowa, in 1887. During the late 1880s and early 1890s the APA waged a widespread lobbying campaign for public control of parochial schools. By the mid-1890s, however, the increasing secularism of American society and the inclusion of some second- and third-generation ethnics in a broadened native-born majority muted the anti-Catholic element in nativist rhetoric but did not relieve all Protestant Americans of suspicions that "Romanism" was a potential threat to the American way of life.

The unpredictability of the business cycle and the apparent hopelessness of solving the problems of urban poverty, crime, and political corruption reinforced the *fin-de-siècle* pessimism of American intellectual elites. The mood that prevailed in fashionable men's clubs and faculty lounges during the 1890s was characterized by a sense that the American people were losing their ability to cope with the developments of modern life. Contemporary jingoistic imperialism and the belief that the United States would have to be strong to make a bid for world power stimulated fears about dissipating national vitality. Reluctant to question American institutions and the fundamental social order, native observers willingly attributed the nation's weaknesses to the alien influences of European immigrants and their U.S.-born descendants. Although natives characteristically magnified the relative dimensions of the influx, there was in fact an increasing proportion of newcomers during the 1880s and 1890s from southern and eastern Europe. Labeled as Slavs, Mediterraneans, or Semites, this component of the European immigration was accused of importing hereditary weaknesses that would undermine the American character. Urban progressives, disgruntled with the languid pace of social and political reform, easily resorted to the excuse that the foreign-born were hopelessly impoverished mentally, physically, and morally and that their presence stymied the improvement of American life.

The New Immigration and the Drive for Restriction

This interpretation of ethnic character served no set of Americans better than the Brahmin, or upper-class, intellectuals of the Northeast. Disturbed by their impotence in modern commercial and political life, they rested their waning claims to social dominance upon cultural and moral leadership. The growth of a cosmopolitan and multiethnic urban culture and the frustrations encountered by genteel urban reformers made these claims extremely shaky. It was easy for them to attribute the receding influence of their class in American life to the proportional decline of a properly appreciative population of Anglo-Saxon stock. The stereotypes of the vulgar Jewish parvenu and the shirt-sleeved Italian laborer represented all that was going awry in American life.

The formation of the Immigration Restriction League in Boston in 1893 was the logical outcome of upper-class ruminations about the sources of national distress.

Jewish immigrants and their descendants, in particular, became targets upon which traditional elites, urban businessmen, and rural conservatives could focus their fears and discontents during the 1890s and later. Rather remarkable economic success in the late 19th and 20th centuries stimulated some American Jews to seek commensurate social recognition. Newly arrived Jews, first from Germany and later from eastern Europe, put their entrepreneurial talents aggressively to work, seeking both economic and social mobility. To Brahmin intellectuals these developments symbolized the collapse of a traditional social order which valued heritage, breeding, and community service above mere wealth and its display. Middle-class businessmen and professionals increasingly found themselves in direct competition with a distinctive ethnic group that displayed impressive commercial and professional talents, a competition that followed them home from office or shop once successful Jews began seeking residences in "better" neighborhoods. For small-town and rural Americans, who had little to fear in the way of economic and social competition with Jewish immigrants, the Jew nonetheless conveniently represented the threat of the godless, industrial city and the control that the distant forces of the financier and the corporation appeared to be exercising over their lives.

Rather than admiring the success of members of the Jewish community in seizing on the opportunities offered by the American economic and social system, old-stock citizens seemed more inclined to believe that Jews used devious methods to warp the system for their exclusive advantage, thus divesting American economic individualism of its supposed ethical restraints. The anti-Semitism that resulted produced a mottled pattern of discrimination in colleges, clubs, resorts, and hotels before the end of the century aimed at denying American Jews the fruits of their material achievement. Later, in the years just before World War I, more systematic attempts to regulate Jewish access to education and employment would deny equality of opportunity even more blatantly.

In the years around the turn of the 20th century, American nationalism became inextricably bound with a pseudoscientific "Anglo-Saxonism." The persistence of ethnic subcultures stimulated fears about the ability of American society to assimilate immigrants and about the capacity of immigrants to effectively acculturate. At the same time a heightened level of international competition raised popular questions about America's unity and strength. In this environment, the idea that only immigrants ethnically harmonious with the nation's Anglo-Saxon core could safely be welcomed into the republican polity grew more attractive. It was only a short step from defensive Anglo-Saxonism, which decried the declining dominance of traditional cultural values, to nativist racism. To the extent that immigrants failed to conform to American values and folkways, they were increasingly labeled not merely alien but biologically inferior. The belief that the United States was being flooded by the defeated members of beaten "races" fitted in neatly with contemporary social Darwinism. The same aversion to racial blending that prevented the United States from incorporating the brown inhabitants of its new Caribbean and South Seas protectorates into a unified empire at the end of the 19th century was played out at home in hostility to tawny Italians and raven-haired immigrant Jews. Southern notables in particular expressed fears that the influx of swarthy "new" immigrants might breach their region's color line, producing untold horrors.

Among federal policy makers, pseudoscientific racism made considerable headway during the last years of the 19th century and the first of the 20th. Congressional approval of a literacy-test qualification for immigrants in 1896 was the logical outgrowth of a reformism that sought "scientific" answers to social problems. The bill was vetoed by President

Cleveland, but the houses of Congress periodically reconsidered the measure and finally overrode Woodrow Wilson's veto on the eve of the U.S. entry into World War I. Congress itself contributed to the popularization of racialist nativism by appointment of a blue-ribbon panel to examine the immigration "problem" in 1907. The Dillingham Commission's report of 1910 concluded that newcomers could be divided into "old" and "new" components, defined by ethnicity and geographic origins. It suggested that the "new" immigrants fitted much less readily into the American society and economy than the "old." Although the voluminous study accurately documented the shift in the national sources of immigration, it failed to take into account differences between specific ethnic groups and made unfair distinctions between the characteristics of the wave of new immigrants, still at its crest, and those of the "old" immigrants who faced examination after an extended history of acculturation and upward mobility. Intelligence tests administered by the armed forces during World War I seemed to confirm for federal officials what Madison Grant had revealed to the country in 1916 in *The Passing of a Great Race*, namely, that the moral, intellectual, and physical tone of the American people was being undermined by continued accretions of inferior "racial" stock. When immigration restriction was finally accomplished during the 1920s, it reflected these considerations. By giving strong preference to arrivals from the northwestern European sources of the "old" immigration, the legislation demonstrated the influence of a racial interpretation of ethnic differences.

The fine points of anti-immigrant racism were sufficiently complex to limit the number of its enthusiasts. But its influence among the nation's urban upper classes was paralleled by a resurgence of cultural tribalism among less sophisticated native-born Americans. Seeking a way to express their continued suspicion of urban, industrial society, country folk chastised immigrant Catholics and Jews as baleful influences upon American life. A reconstituted Ku Klux Klan merged anti-Catholicism, anti-Semitism, and Protestant fundamentalism to wage a vigorous rearguard defense of a passing American way of life. Inspired by the nationalist visions of Georgian William Simmons, the Klan took on an increasingly nativistic tone in the years after its founding in 1915 and became a genuine mass movement during the 1920s.

Ethnocultural biases grew during World War I. Resentful of imperial Germany's challenge to world order and prosperity, many Americans demanded ruthless elimination of all traces of German culture in American life. Once the United States had entered the conflict, however, the spirit of national unity that suffused the nation temporarily discouraged criticism of other ethnic groups. Wartime prosperity defused interethnic economic competition and made immigrant labor seem a valuable strategic asset. But in their zeal for a united front against the enemy, the native-born increasingly demanded the full acculturation of newcomers as proof of loyalty. The "100 percent Americanism" campaign that extended through the war years displayed the considerable intolerance of the American people for ethnic cultures and a patriotically inspired disinclination to see much virtue in cultural pluralism.

Developments in the immediate postwar world did nothing to persuade Americans to adopt a more cosmopolitan outlook on ethnic diversity. An abrupt slide into economic recession exacerbated old fears about immigration and overexpansion of the labor force. What was worse, the deteriorating economic situation was punctuated by strikes and labor unrest. Despite their relative weakness, radical labor organizations like the IWW (Industrial Workers of the World) which sought fundamental changes in the American economic system attracted excessive public attention and terrified the native-born middle class. The success of the Communist revolution in Russia and the rapid emergence of the Soviet Union as a European power reinforced the idea that an international conspiracy was afoot to undermine traditional Western liberalism. Scattered terrorist bombing incidents during 1919 encouraged the popular hysteria known as the Red Scare. Native-born Americans easily transferred their wartime hostility to Germans to central and eastern European ethnic populations in the United States, on the grounds that they were propagators of radicalism and un-American ideologies. The assimilationist goal of 100 percent Americanism disappeared in the face of renewed feeling that many immigrants were incapable of understanding republican principles or of taking on the virtues of the loyal, progressive American.

When Congress passed a national origins system of immigration restriction in 1921, it was a logical culmination to the antiradical, anti-Catholic, and racialist strains of American nativism. By closing off much of the influx of immigrants from outside northwestern Europe and the British Isles, the Percentage Immigration Law met most popular demands for a solution to the immigration question without appearing overtly xenophobic. The gates remained open to culturally and ethnically "harmonious" immigrants, preserving the idea that American society was sufficiently resilient to accept newcomers into its midst. Restriction was moved from an emergency to a permanent basis by the Johnson-Reed Act of 1924.

Since the 1920s

The immediate effect of immigration restriction was to eliminate much of the excuse for contemporary excesses of ethnic bigotry. Without a clear goal to sustain it, antiforeign sentiment subsided. During the 1920s anti-Catholicism remained an effective vehicle of rural resentment against the sinful cities, merging nicely with Protestant fundamentalism and prohibitionist sentiment, a fact not without consequence in the 1928 presidential campaign of Alfred E. Smith. Likewise, anti-Semitism served to place national problems upon "foreign" shoulders. In general, however, the slower growth of

American ethnic groups occasioned by immigration restriction encouraged the acculturation if not the complete assimilation of immigrants and their children. In turn, acculturation removed some of the more visible irritants to American ethnic relations. The shared trials of the Great Depression and World War II were unifying experiences in American life, and the excesses of Nazi Germany brought both racial and religious prejudice into popular disrepute. Cracks in the national-origins program of immigration admissions appeared as early as the mid-1930s when federal authorities permitted the entrance of limited numbers of nonquota European political refugees, a practice that was continued during and after the war.

Nevertheless, ethnic prejudice has not disappeared from American society in the second half of the 20th century. Clumsy forms of institutional discrimination, such as the Jewish quotas maintained by some private schools and universities before World War II, are gone; but some inhibitors to true equality of opportunity for members of American ethnic groups remain. Distinctive ethnic class and occupational characteristics in modern urban society are partly products of persistent differences in group values, goals, and economic strategies. As such, they suggest the actual limits of the acculturation and homogenization of American ethnic groups. But differential employment patterns also point to the persistence of interethnic biases that restrict the access of some citizens to a full range of occupational alternatives.

After World War II, genuine meritocracies oblivious to ethnicity took shape in some of the nation's more prestigious professions, providing new outlets for the skills and ambitions of talented members of white ethnic groups. Immigrants and their descendants also effectively utilized positions of influence in labor unions and municipal politics to provide paths of mobility for manual and clerical workers. What were initially refuges from oppression for some ethnic groups paradoxically have become sources of power and group advancement. In fact, some ethnic leaders now assert that efforts to "reform" big-city machine politics and to impose racial quotas upon labor unions are nothing less than assaults by "WASP" Americans upon the primary avenues of ethnic social mobility and hence are ill-disguised forms of discrimination. Of all areas of American occupational life, the management hierarchies of industrial corporations have perhaps been the most difficult for white ethnic groups to enter. In corporate life, where cronyism and conformity are keys to advancement, exclusion of ethnoreligious minorities from certain kinds of clubs, lodges, and social circles has proven an impediment to occupational mobility. To a considerable extent, ethnicity has become bound with class as a social identifier in 20th-century America. The tendency of Americans to evaluate the social worth of individuals primarily in economic terms has rewarded those who are able to take advantage of available paths of social mobility, but it may also reinforce the remnants of ethnic prejudice with class bias.

Conclusion

For white Americans, culture has been the crux of ethnic difference, and ethnocentrism the enduring form of hostility met by ethnic minorities. Efforts to attribute the cultural proclivities of immigrants to heredity or to make fundamentally physical distinctions between white ethnic minorities have repeatedly failed. The adaptability of European immigrants to the outward forms of American life stymied attempts to prove that culture and achievement were contingent upon birth. Bolder ventures at differentiating white ethnic stocks on the basis of physical characteristics alone ran headlong into the essential similarity of Caucasian types. The elimination of even superficially distinctive physical features remained possible in the absence of effective prohibitive taboos against white ethnic amalgamation. The perception and meaning of ethnocultural differences among white Americans has been bound inextricably with the incentives for interethnic hostility. Developments in American political life, foreign relations, and intellectual or popular culture are what have invested particular ethnic characteristics with meaning. During the mid-19th century, while the American as a distinctive national type was still in the process of development, native-born Anglo-Americans regarded religion, tradition, and folkways as the determinants of nationality and heartily despised immigrants for introducing an unwanted cultural pluralism to the United States. At times in America's past when old-stock native-born citizens felt threatened by foreign enemies, they focused their concern specifically upon the elements of newcomers' political culture which could be construed as antithetical to republicanism. In periods of intense interparty political rivalry, nativist partisans emphasized the deficiencies of education, intelligence, and morality among ethnic voters.

When white ethnic groups have grown so large or locally concentrated as to challenge the economic, political, or social predominance of old-stock Americans, the motives for nativistic prejudice have been palpably transformed. Interethnic competition in the form of a conflict of material interests invests ethnocultural characteristics with primarily symbolic significance. Rather than appearing immediate threats to native values and traditions, they become mere tags to identify social competitors. Toward the end of the 19th century, ethnicity became only one of the multiple sources of American personal identity, taking its place among class, occupation, residence, and associational memberships. Old-stock Americans were especially prone to link ethnicity and social class; ethnicity had the advantage of being an optional social identity which could be selectively applied. Because few physical marks revealed the nature of white ancestry, an indelible and stigmatizing ethnicity was attributed only to Americans outside the pale of respectability—the Roman Catholic, the socialist, the urban delinquent. For members of ethnic groups who conformed to Anglo-American values and pursued an approved lifestyle, ethnicity in many cases could be dropped by choice.

Because of the permeability of ethnic boundaries within white America, it has been difficult for the native-born to institutionalize interethnic discrimination to keep immigrants and their descendants from challenging Anglo-American social predominance. Attempts to restrict the franchise to native-born citizens during the 19th century were made difficult by the invisibility of many white ethnic-group members and by intensive rivalry in American politics that made the major parties eager to attract immigrant votes. As full-fledged participants in the American political system, immigrants and their descendants acquired sufficient influence to prevent most other kinds of publicly sponsored ethnic bias. De facto discrimination against immigrants, especially in the form of residential segregation, actually had the effect of concentrating ethnic populations and giving them disproportionate political influence. Though the extraordinary convergence of nativistic prejudices during the 1920s made it impossible to halt the drive for immigration restriction, the members of ethnic groups already on American soil could expect relatively equal treatment under the laws of the United States. In the U.S. open-market economy, the value of immigrants as producers and consumers ensured that ethnic minorities could hold prosperity hostage against overzealous nativistic bias. Contemporary enthusiasm for rediscovering ethnic roots and reconstructing ethnic communities as a bulwark against the anomie of modern middle-class life illustrates the extent to which ethnic-group affiliation has now become a positive optional identity in American life.

Despite all the changes that have occurred, the situation of blacks in American society since the 18th century has been characterized by certain continuities that help set them apart from all other groups. Whereas other racially distinctive minorities, such as American Indians and Asians, have been differentiated as often by their traditional cultures as by their physical characteristics, blacks have consistently been defined solely as a racial group. Furthermore, a peculiar conception of black ethnicity dictates that an individual with any known African ancestry is considered to be a black person, whatever his actual pigmentation or sociocultural characteristics. Hence, identification with the Afro-American community has been involuntary to a greater extent than have memberships in other ethnic groups. The taboo against miscegenation and the implied fear of "pollution" from the incorporation of anyone with black ancestry into white primary groups have remained strong despite the demise of antimiscegenation statutes. Intergroup mobility by people of mixed white-Indian or white-Asian ancestry has not, at least in recent times, raised comparable anxieties. Hence there are grounds for concern that a peculiar and exacting sense of difference, based on an implicit assumption of hereditary taint, may be an enduring element of black-white relations in the United States. But a sense of difference is only one of the preconditions for unequal treatment of blacks. Economic incentives for consigning blacks to lower-class status have proved of varying strength in different historical situations, and there is reason to believe that the transformation of most blacks from rural dependents to enfranchised competitors in the urban industrial labor market has reduced the profits of discrimination. The ability of blacks to force important concessions from the white majority has also varied over time; and the power differential, whether calculated in political or economic terms, has been greatly reduced since the Great Depression. If history is any guide, one might be inclined to predict that strong prejudices will survive so long as the black community remains an involuntary racial group rather than a voluntary ethnic community, but that elimination of the most damaging forms of discrimination is nevertheless possible within the foreseeable future.

3

EFFORTS AGAINST PREJUDICE

Prejudice and discrimination against racial and ethnic groups are major strands in the history of the American people. Another strand, initially tenuous and shaky but which has grown in the past 15 years to equal strength, is the effort of law to control or eradicate discrimination and its effects. The history of this effort is closely entwined with the history of the largest racially defined minority group in the United States: blacks. A great body of law supported their enslavement in the southern states and their civil inferiority in the North. But in the early 19th century reformers launched a countertradition of law, which attempted to assure equality for blacks. Before the Civil War this body of law was very weak and was limited to the North. The Emancipation Proclamation and the postwar constitutional amendments and Civil Rights Acts caused enormous changes in the legal position of blacks. The high point in this national effort to achieve equality was reached in 1875. Thereafter, national political reconciliation and restrictive Supreme Court judgments marked a withdrawal. Many of the achievements of the Reconstruction were lost. Aside from the historic elimination of slavery, the political, economic, and social position of blacks showed little change in the South, where the great majority lived.

There was, however, a Second Reconstruction. Its beginnings may be variously located. One was in the educational and political activities of the Negro defense organizations, principally the National Association for the Advancement of Colored People (NAACP), fighting the most outrageous of the conditions that kept blacks down—unpunished lynchings, poll taxes and other means of denying the vote, the closing of higher education opportunities to blacks in the South. In the late 1930s the Supreme Court began to erode the barriers to opportunity in higher education. The New Deal, expanding greatly the role of the federal government, and based on the rising power of second-generation immigrants and the labor movement, was another source of the Second Reconstruction. It brought to blacks in the South an awareness that federal law could improve their condition. The Second World War was a third source: waged against Nazi Germany, it embarrassed American racists and emboldened those who opposed them. The Second Reconstruction proper may be dated to the historic *Brown* decision of the Supreme Court in 1954 which struck down the "separate but equal" principle in education. It reached its climax with the black protest movement led by Martin Luther King, Jr., and the adoption of strong civil rights legislation in 1964 and 1965. In the years since, as the administration of laws against discrimination has become a major task of federal government, there has been growing debate as to the proper character and future direction of this effort.

The Second Reconstruction has ended; three major outcomes distinguish it from the ending of the First Reconstruction. First, powerful government agencies have been established, employing thousands of people and spending hundreds of millions of dollars, whose permanent task is to fight discrimination and achieve equality for minority groups. Second, blacks and other minorities are now fully enfranchised, play a major role in government, and form a permanent support for the fight against discrimination. Third, the movement against discrimination now embraces other major ethnic groups, especially Mexican-Americans, Puerto Ricans, and other Latin Americans, but also American Indians, Asians, and nonethnic groups such as women and the handicapped, augmenting its political strength even while introducing certain conflicts among all those who now benefit from antidiscrimination law.

As part of the history of discrimination, then, we must furnish some account of the efforts to overcome discrimination. This discussion focuses on the attempts to achieve equality for blacks, but those efforts were directed to a universal purpose, with the result that other groups could participate in and benefit from them. It was not blacks alone who were guaranteed "the equal protection of the laws" in various respects, just as it was not blacks alone who had suffered from their unequal application. The Chinese and Japanese in particular had been subjected to fierce discriminatory legislation. American Indians present a more complex picture. Although law was intended to preserve their special and separate status, it was also applied without their participation, in ignorance of their needs, and with a good deal of prejudice. Their special status made difficult any simple application of the principle of equal protection, for their interests also required the defense of their unique legal position.

Because the attack on discrimination emphasized the equality of races, laws designed to keep down Chinese and Japanese fell before it along with those designed to keep down blacks. The story of the legal battle against discrimination should deal with many groups besides blacks. But because this battle is integrally linked with blacks as the central concern of efforts to overcome discrimination, they are also the chief subject of this account.

The process cannot be divorced from the larger movements of American history. The American Revolution produced some reaction in the abolition of slavery in northern states, and in many of them the assumption by free Negroes of civil and political rights. But this was a weak echo. The Civil War created a much broader and more active response, even though its hopes were not fulfilled. Finally, the New Deal and World War II, with their promises of social and racial equality, began a movement of political pressure and protest and of executive, legislative, and judicial response, which has become institutionalized, and around which conflict continues. This conflict, however, is not over whether equality should prevail, but over how best to achieve it.

Before the Civil War

The social position of the Negro in the free northern states before the Civil War evoked the first organized efforts to establish municipal laws prohibiting discrimination on the basis of race or descent. These states had abolished slavery by 1820 and politically opposed its expansion; civil equality there became a practical issue a half-century before the debates in Congress during Reconstruction over the rights of newly emancipated southern blacks.

The framers of the U.S. Constitution had omitted any reference to special or separate treatment of free blacks or other races, with the result that northern state policy-makers perceived no constitutional barriers to laws that imposed civil disabilities on Negroes and denied them most of the rights enjoyed by white citizens. Legislators and jurists in the North, though explicitly opposed to the form of Negro slavery practiced in the South, pursued policies of white supremacy in social and political life. They were guided by the prevailing assumption that custom and race had assigned blacks to an inferior social position which neither statute nor judicial decision could alter; a social commentator in the 1820s noted that "chains of a stronger kind manacled their limbs, from which no legislative act could free them; a mental and moral subordination and inferiority to which tyrant custom has here subjected all the sons and daughters of Africa." Democratic, Federalist, and Whig politicians passed state laws that barred blacks from the professions and skilled trades, and enforced segregation in public accommodations and transportation facilities. In New England, local school committees created separate schools for blacks; the state of New York authorized school districts to establish segregated educational facilities. Pennsylvania and Ohio required separate schools for blacks wherever accommodations could be provided for 20 or more students; and some midwestern and western states prohibited black children from attending public schools at all.

During the 1820s and 1830s, when Jacksonian Democrats were redrafting state constitutions to expand the political rights of adult white males and widen the suffrage, the political rights of blacks in northern states were drastically contracting. By 1840 the states in which over 90 percent of all northern Negroes resided had legally extinguished or practically abrogated their voting and office-holding rights. New Jersey, Pennsylvania, and Connecticut rescinded laws that had given Negroes the franchise; New York permitted them the vote only if they met specific property-holding and residency requirements that were not imposed on whites. Only in Massachusetts, Vermont, New Hampshire, and Maine, where few Negroes resided, could they exercise political rights on an equal basis with adult white males.

Most of the free northern states before the Civil War also deprived blacks, through law or practice, of fundamental judicial rights. Negro testimony in cases involving a white person was banned by Illinois, Indiana, Ohio, Iowa, and California; Oregon laws prohibited Negroes from filing lawsuits.

That northern blacks could be denied equal treatment with whites was justified constitutionally by what Andrew Jackson's attorney general, John Berrien, in 1831 called the "general right of a State to regulate persons of color within its own limits . . . recognized by the [state police-power proviso of the] tenth amendment." Many policy-makers also argued that the Constitution gave state governments sole authority to define the civil rights of state citizens and to prescribe separate sets of rights and privileges for different classes of citizens.

The growth of an organized movement to abolish slavery within the United States stimulated the first attempt to change discriminatory laws in the North. This movement was particularly successful in Massachusetts. Beginning in the early 1830s abolitionists, reformers, and Negroes repeatedly petitioned the Massachusetts legislature to repeal its law prohibiting interracial marriages, to terminate segregation in public transportation, and to create racially integrated school systems throughout the state. Their campaign began to achieve concrete results in the 1840s. A legislative committee of the state House of Representatives investigated complaints against the interracial marriage ban, and warned in 1840 that if Massachusetts continued to retain its antimiscegenation law it would "virtually assert [Negro] inequality, and justify that theory of negro slavery which represents it as a state of necessary tutelage and guardianship." Sensitive to the charge that the law was inconsistent with their opposition to slavery, Massachusetts legislators repealed it in 1843.

The strategy of abolitionists in their attack on segregated public transportation was initially to obtain a court injunction against separate facilities. Failing to achieve this, they pressed the state legislature to guarantee equal treatment of the races. A joint legislative committee found that segregation in railroad cars, steamboats, and stagecoaches violated the state constitution and recommended that segregation in public transportation on the basis of descent, sect, or color should not be permitted. This bill was defeated, but the railroads bowed to the pressure of antislavery groups and voluntarily abolished segregation in their cars and stations in the mid-1840s. Frederick Douglass (c. 1817–1895), an ex-slave who became the outstanding Negro leader of the abolitionist movement, had been a vocal critic of segregated railroad lines. He remarked in 1849 that "not a single railroad can be found in any part of Massachusetts, where a colored man is treated and esteemed in any other light than that of a man and a traveler."

The opponents of discrimination devoted greater energy to achieving equal access for Negroes to public schools, a goal which many saw as the fundamental step toward establishing a more harmonious society and fostering the social progress of blacks. Douglass, who rated equal opportunity in education as a higher priority than the achievement of full political equality, wrote: "Contact on equal terms is the best means to abolish caste. *It is caste abolished.* With Equal Suffrage, 13,675 black men come into contact [with whites] on equal terms, for ten minutes once a year, at the polls; with equal school rights, 15,778 colored children and youth come in contact on equal terms with white children and youth, three hundred days in the year, and from six to ten hours each day. And these children, in a few years, become the people of the state."

By 1845 abolitionists had secured the desegregation of the public school systems of Salem, New Bedford, Nantucket, Worcester, and Lowell. Boston's schools became the target of legal suits brought by black parents joined by the Massachusetts Anti-Slavery Society, which urged "friends of the cause" to provide Negroes with "all possible aid in securing the full and equal enjoyment of the public schools." Benjamin Roberts, whose daughter had been denied admission four times to a white primary school located in the school district where the Roberts family resided, obtained as legal counsel Charles Sumner, the anti-slavery U.S. Senator from Massachusetts, and filed a civil suit in the state Superior Court against the Boston Primary School Committee. Chief Justice Lemuel Shaw, speaking for a unanimous court, stated flatly that the school committee had discharged its responsibility to black citizens by providing their children with adequate, albeit segregated, facilities. Shaw rejected the plaintiff's contention that segregated facilities instilled in the populace the notion of black inferiority.

Negro civic leaders and parents established the Equal School Rights Committee to end segregated schools in Boston by legislation, and after five years of lobbying, public rallies, and aggressive publicity the city's committee on public instruction in 1854 recommended to the mayor and board of aldermen that the segregated schools be abolished. Before Boston could act, the state legislature in 1855 passed a law prohibiting the use of racial or religious distinctions in the admission of students to public schools in Massachusetts. The first state statute to outlaw racially discriminatory practices in a public institution was thus enacted on the eve of the Civil War. Massachusetts was also the first state to allow blacks to serve as jurors. It was not until 1860, however, after five years of intensive lobbying and publicity by abolitionists and blacks, that the first Negro jurymen were named in Worcester.

The hard-won gains of Massachusetts blacks heartened Negroes and social reformers in other free states. In 1849 Ohio bowed to the agitation of abolitionists and eliminated its ban against judicial testimony by blacks. In Rhode Island a bill prohibiting segregation in public schools missed passage by only two votes. In the 1850s Negroes brought civil suits in state courts to desegregate public schools in Ohio and Indiana, but these courts held that separate schools for blacks and whites were legitimate so long as they supplied equal educational opportunities.

Civil War and Reconstruction

The legal principles calling for equal treatment and due process can be invoked against prejudice and discriminatory treatment independently of political power. But effective change without power is rare. In the *Dred Scott* case of 1857 the U.S. Supreme Court declared federal laws prohibiting slavery in the territories unconstitutional. This decision did not stand long, for it was one of the events that precipitated the Civil War. And with the military defeat of the South, one of the first acts of Congress was to pass the Thirteenth Amendment, prohibiting slavery.

The destruction of the power of the southern slave states set the stage for an unprecedented expansion of federal jurisdiction and the establishment of a polity anchored in a common national citizenship for blacks and whites—and, by implication, for all races. It was the task of the 39th and 40th congresses, which met from December 1865 to March 1869, to define the civil status of millions of emancipated southern blacks as well as that of blacks in the North. Clashing repeatedly with President Andrew Johnson, a Tennesseean with firm views on the inferiority of Negroes, the Republican Congress enacted the first federal Civil Rights Act in 1866. This authorized the continued operation of the wartime Freedman's Bureau which assisted ex-slaves, declared all persons born in the United States to be American citizens, and established that all citizens "of every race and color, without regard to any previous condition of slavery or involuntary servitude," should have the same personal, property, and civil rights in every state and territory "as is enjoyed by white citizens." Moreover, any person who deprived another, on account of race or color, of civil rights enumerated in the act became guilty of a federal crime. The bill was passed over Johnson's veto.

Fearful of an adverse Supreme Court judgment on the constitutionality of the 1866 Civil Rights Act, Congress drafted the Fourteenth Amendment (ratified in 1868) which incorporated the principal elements of the 1866 legislation and extended the scope of federal protection to "citizens of the United States": no state could abridge their "privileges or immunities" or "deprive any person of life, liberty, or property, without due process of law" or "deny to any person within its jurisdiction the equal protection of the laws."

The forceful wording of the amendment affirmed a national policy of equality before the law for all races, but the degree and nature of the protection secured under federal law were subject to judicial interpretation. "What was meant by these phrases," one historian remarked, "would be the major issue in American constitutional law for the next century and more." Although the Fourteenth Amendment was a step toward expanded federal protection, it sought this objective by limiting the powers of states to interfere with broadly phrased rights rather than by positive extension of federal authority. Where federal jurisdiction ended and state jurisdiction began would be the thorniest question challenging the interpreters of the Fourteenth Amendment in the years ahead.

The Fifteenth Amendment in 1869 prohibited the federal or state governments from denying the right to vote "on account of race, color, or previous condition of servitude." Time proved, however, that discrimination in voting rights on grounds of race alone did not rule out other forms of discrimination which deprived blacks of the vote. The Fifteenth Amendment was buttressed by the Civil Rights Acts of 1870 and 1871, which made the deliberate obstruction of Negro suffrage a high federal crime punishable by a severe fine.

Although the Reconstruction congressional legislation expressed a powerful impulse to create a new and equal civil status for blacks, the motives of northern policy-makers were mixed, for many did not accept the equality of the races. Such progressive Republican leaders as Lyman Trumbull of Illinois and John Sherman of Ohio believed unquestioningly in the natural inferiority of the Negro; and many prominent congressional Republicans hoped to improve the conditions of blacks in the South chiefly in order to ward off a massive migration to the northern states. Republican support for the Civil Rights Act of 1866 rested in part on the popular view expressed by a Republican lawyer from Illinois: "It would be unwise to allow the negro to vote in Illinois and not in the South. The result of that would be to make Illinois a negro Mecca." Indeed, at the end of the Civil War, Negroes were still denied suffrage in 18 out of 25 states in the North. The majority of northern states maintained segregated public facilities and sanctioned restrictions on the residence and employment opportunities of blacks. From 1865 to 1868 voters in Connecticut, Ohio, Wisconsin, Michigan, Kansas, and Missouri rejected in popular referenda proposed amendments to their state constitutions that would have granted the franchise to Negroes.

The great majority of the states, however, chose to endorse the Fourteenth and Fifteenth amendments; the state platforms of the Republican party in the late 1860s were filled with glowing expressions of racial equality. Iowa's Republican platform stated in 1866: "The first and highest duty of our free Government is to secure to all its citizens, regardless of race, religion, or color, equality before the law, equal protection from it, equal responsibility to it." Minnesota Republicans declared that "the measure of a man's political rights should be neither his religion, his birthplace, his race, his color, nor any merely physical characteristics."

From 1865 into the 1870s a few states began to enact laws prohibiting racial discrimination. In 1865 Massachusetts became the first state to outlaw distinctions or restrictions based on race among patrons of licensed places of public accommodation. New York passed in 1874 its first civil rights law, prohibiting racial discrimination in theaters, inns, cemeteries, public conveyances, places of amusement or entertainment, and public institutions of learning. In the same year Kansas became the third state to pass an antidiscrimination law, similar to that of New York.

Black civic organizations and lobbying groups were important agents in the creation of more progressive local and national policies in the field of civil rights. State conventions of Negro civic leaders, such as the Illinois State Convention of Colored Men held in 1866, and smaller city conventions, developed surveys "to thoroughly canvass the subject of the disabilities, educational and political, that dwell on persons of color . . . and to devise and set in motion effective agencies for the permanent removal of the same." Negroes in Kansas established civil rights clubs and an equal rights association that played a major role in securing the Kansas antidiscrimination law of 1874.

The omnibus Civil Rights Act proposed by Charles Sumner in May 1870 and passed by Congress in March 1875 marked the zenith of the post-bellum movement to achieve civil rights for blacks. In its original form the bill prohibited unequal treatment of the races in "railroads, steamboats, public conveyances, hotels, licensed theatres, houses of public entertainment, common schools, and institutions of learning authorized by law, church institutions, and cemetery associations incorporated by national or state authority; also on juries in courts, national and state." The Senate Judiciary Committee refused to report the bill out. Shortly after he reintroduced it in December 1873, Sumner died. His supporters, some of them Negro members of Congress, pressed for the bill's passage. However, a significant change in rank-and-file Republican support for civil rights legislation had been developing: some feared the consequences of federally ordered school desegregation, others were offended by the inclusion of churches, and still others opposed the extension of federal control over public transportation.

The long debate over the controversial measure revealed the conception of racial equality held by proponents of the Civil Rights Act. J. H. Rainey, a black congressman from South Carolina, repeatedly denied the charge of the bill's opponents that it would produce "social equality" of the races through coercion. Rainey stressed that the bill would ensure only a common access to public facilities. "I venture to assert to my white fellow citizens," Rainey said, "that we the colored people are not in quest of social equality. For one I do not ask to be introduced into your family circles if you are not yet disposed to receive me there." Congressman Harris of Massachusetts, a supporter of the bill, emphasized that its goal was only to assure common hospitality to all races in public facilities. John Lynch, a Negro congressman from Mississippi, insisted that the bill would give rights "which should be accorded to every citizen alike," not social equality of the races. Again and again the proponents sounded the common theme that the legislation was aimed at securing equal access to public facilities and equal civil rights, not equality of social conditions between the races.

When the Civil Rights Act of 1875 finally passed, key sections of Sumner's original bill that proposed to ban segregated schools and juries were deleted. Even so, the act was still the boldest federal effort to produce civil equality between whites and Negroes. It began with phrases recalling the language of the Declaration of Independence: "Whereas, it is essential to just government we recognize the equality of all men before the law, and hold that it is the duty of government in its dealings with the people to mete out equal and exact justice to all of whatever nationality, race, color, or persuasion, religious or political." The heart of the law guaranteed all persons regardless of race "the full and equal enjoyment of the accommodations, advantages, facilities, and privileges of inns, public conveyances on land or water, theaters, and other places of public amusement."

Next came the struggle in the courts over constitutionality. During the 1870s the Supreme Court affirmed the constitutionality of the civil rights laws of 1866, 1870, and 1871. The first Supreme Court interpretation of the Fourteenth Amendment came in its review of the *Slaughter-House Cases* of 1873.

As a public health measure Louisiana had granted a monopoly to a corporation to operate stockyards, landing places, and a slaughterhouse in New Orleans, and some butchers had filed suit against the state for violating their rights under the Fourteenth Amendment. A five-to-four majority of the Court found against the butchers' contention that the state government's action was prohibited by the privileges and immunities and equal protection clauses of the Fourteenth Amendment, on the ground that the Fourteenth Amendment was intended primarily to protect the newly freed slaves. The majority also held that the amendment protected only the privileges and immunities of "citizens of the United States," that it conferred no new rights upon them, and that these rights were quite limited—for example, the right to free access to subtreasuries and land offices. The Court insisted on a distinction between rights held as a citizen of the United States and those held as a citizen of a state; to interpret the amendment otherwise would make of the Court "a perpetual censor upon all legislation of the states, on the civil rights of their own citizens," and would produce a federal tyranny. In order to challenge state infringements on his rights, a citizen had to appeal to the state legislature or state courts. The implications for the civil rights of Negroes were tremendous, for this decision kept public education and public accommodations under state authority. With civil rights defined largely as issuing from the legislative power and judicial authority of state governments, victims of discriminatory local laws could not obtain the protection of the federal government.

A decade after the *Slaughter-House Cases* decision, the Supreme Court reviewed together seven cases which involved challenges to the constitutionality of the 1875 Civil Rights Act requiring nondiscrimination in public accommodation and facilities. The spirit of the civil rights cause had faltered by the 1880s, and the Supreme Court judgment dealt it a mortal blow. The core of the plaintiffs' arguments was that the Thirteenth Amendment had empowered Congress to pass all laws necessary for the eradication of slavery with all "its badges and incidents," and that exclusion from accommodations in public facilities amounted to the imposition of a "badge of slavery." Justice Joseph Bradley, writing for the majority, denied that refusal or denial of accommodation had no connection with involuntary servitude: "It would be running the slavery argument into the ground to make it apply to every act of discrimination which a person may see fit to make as to the guests he will entertain, or as to the people he will take into his coach or cab or car, or admit to his concert or theater." Bradley affirmed the constitutionality of the Thirteenth and Fourteenth amendments and the

Civil Rights Acts of 1866, 1870, and 1871, but declared the 1875 Civil Rights Act unconstitutional. It violated the Tenth Amendment grant of authority to states for "the enforcement and vindication of all rights of life, liberty, and property" and attempted also to regulate private acts. This was only the third time in history that the Supreme Court had invalidated congressional legislation—a step it had taken in *Marbury* v. *Madison* (1803) and *Dred Scott* (1857).

Justice John Marshall Harlan wrote a vigorous dissent in which he argued that "keepers of inns, and managers of places of public amusement are agents or instrumentalities of the state, because they are charged with duties to the public, and are amenable, in respect of their duties and functions, to government regulation."

Although the Supreme Court in the late 19th century adopted an extremely narrow interpretation of the civil rights protected by the Fourteenth Amendment, it did extend to other groups the limited protections that it recognized. Chinese Americans emigrating to California in the 1850s had been subjected to discrimination by both extralegal action and positive legislation. Here the Fourteenth Amendment was held to apply to protect others besides blacks. In *Yick Wo* v. *Hopkins* (1886) the Court ruled that a municipal law prohibiting the operation of laundries in wooden buildings was unconstitutional because it discriminated without legitimate reason or cause against Chinese laundry owners as a class. Between 1885 and 1895 the Supreme Court in four separate decisions consistently affirmed that differential treatment of separate classifications of persons could satisfy the Fourteenth Amendment's equal protection proviso only when such classification was based reasonably on substantial differences "pertinent to valid legislative objectives" and when it was applied equally to all persons in a specific classification. Even the Court's decision in *Plessy* v. *Ferguson* (1896), declaring segregation in public conveyances legal because of the authority of state governments to pass laws regulating the rights of its citizens, stressed that equality of accommodations was the sine qua non of constitutionality under the equal protection clause. What was established in *Plessy* was the constitutionality of separate but *equal* facilities.

What the majority refused to recognize, as Justice Harlan pointed out in a historic dissent, was that segregation led inevitably to *unequal* conditions, thus making Negroes an inferior caste and whites "a dominant race, a superior class of citizens." Harlan asserted that the majority decision would one day seem as "pernicious" as the *Dred Scott* ruling and would "render permanent peace impossible and . . . keep alive a conflict of races, the continuance of which must do harm to all concerned."

From the End of Reconstruction to the New Deal

To fill the vacuum left by the retreat of the federal government, many state legislatures passed antidiscrimination statutes modeled on the ill-fated Civil Rights Act of 1875. Eighteen states in the Northeast, the Midwest, and Far West established codes by 1900 outlawing discrimination in public places for reasons of race or color. Massachusetts (1865), New York (1874), and Kansas (1874) had already done so. Connecticut, Iowa, New Jersey, and Ohio enacted similar statutes in 1884; Rhode Island, Michigan, Illinois, Indiana, Minnesota, Nebraska, and Colorado followed in 1885; and so did Washington, Wisconsin, and California in the 1890s.

The state laws were based on common principles and employed a common legal vocabulary. They stipulated that no one could be denied equal privileges and facilities in places of public accommodation on the grounds of race, color (in some states, religion), or previous condition of servitude. Not until the mid-20th century was discrimination on the basis of national origin or ancestry forbidden by state law. Most states enumerated a list of public places in which the antidiscrimination statute was operative. Violators of these laws were subject to criminal sanctions of fine or imprisonment, or civil sanctions which provided remedies to injured parties.

According to the *Slaughter-House* decision and the *Civil Rights Cases* of 1883, the state antidiscrimination laws were within the province of legitimate state police powers. But state judges often limited the application and power of these laws. Thus, on the principle that penal statutes must be strictly construed, the Nebraska Supreme Court ruled in 1889 that because a state antidiscrimination law provided for criminal penalties and ambiguously referred to "citizens" and to "persons," only citizens could claim protection under the law. A New York court in 1917 denied redress to Negroes who sued a New York saloon because a "saloon" was not specifically mentioned among the public places listed in the state law.

In the face of strict interpretations by the courts, state legislators seeking an effective civil rights policy made the list of specifically enumerated public places exhaustive: those specified in the New York civil rights law included over 50 separately identified facilities. In 1913 New York added to its civil rights code a ban on discriminatory advertising of public facilities and accommodations; New Jersey, Maine, Massachusetts, Pennsylvania, Michigan, Wisconsin, Illinois, Colorado, Oregon, and Washington soon followed.

State civil rights laws guaranteeing equal access to public accommodations did not provide strong sanctions for enforcement. Some of the state laws in the early 20th century prescribed the same fine for damages that had been assessed in the 1880s and 1890s. In states where violation of an antidiscrimination law required a criminal trial, the plaintiffs often had to contend with juries as prejudiced as the defendants. The initiative for filing a suit and convincing a public prosecutor or grand jury to act rested with a minority-group member. And civil action required substantial resources.

The efforts of northern state legislators to fill the void left by congressional inaction and the Supreme Court's negativism were without great effect. In the South, on the other hand, the *Civil Rights Cases* decision and *Plessy* v. *Ferguson* opened the way to a massive, legal restriction of the rights of blacks. Jim Crow laws and custom separated the races in every sphere of daily life—schools, colleges and universities, government facilities, places of work, recreation, and amusement, and churches. And the separate facilities provided to blacks were uniformly inferior. Law or custom prevented blacks from voting, participating in the activities of the major (Democratic) party, holding public office, and sitting on juries.

The pattern of segregation and discrimination spread to the federal government; workers in government agencies in Washington, D.C., were segregated, beginning with the U.S. Bureau of the Census under President Taft; under Woodrow Wilson segregation extended to federal civil-service workers in Washington. The few token appointments blacks received from the federal government shrank during the Taft and Wilson administrations. In World War I the army was totally segregated (as had been the Union army in the Civil War). There were only minimal improvements under post–World War I Republican presidents.

The National Association for the Advancement of Colored People, founded in 1910, devoted itself in the 1920s principally to arousing public feeling against lynchings of blacks in the South and to securing passage of a federal antilynching law, in which it did not succeed. It was more successful in the federal courts; in 1917 the Supreme Court declared racial zoning for housing unconstitutional (*Buchanan* v. *Warley*). But other means of restricting blacks and other groups from certain areas, principally the restrictive covenant, remained intact. As early as 1924, in *Nixon* v. *Herndon*, the NAACP succeeded in having a Texas statute forbidding black participation in primaries ruled unconstitutional. But southern states had many other legal mechanisms for restricting black suffrage; although many of these were struck down, legal and extralegal devices still prevented blacks from voting.

The New Deal and World War II

Landmarks in overcoming discrimination during the long presidency of Franklin D. Roosevelt were few. Nevertheless, the New Deal and U.S. participation in World War II undermined segregation and discriminatory treatment. A huge expansion of federal programs in aid of the poor focused specifically on the poorest part of the country with the great majority of blacks: the South. Fashioned by an administration whose electoral support included new immigrant groups, labor, and northern blacks, they were often administered in nondiscriminatory fashion. In some respects they also yielded to the apparently impregnable hold that discriminatory policies had taken on the South. But, as Gunnar Myrdal wrote in *An American Dilemma* in the early 1940s:

> Not overlooking the considerable discrimination against Negroes in the local administration of New Deal measures in the South, we must see that the New Deal has made a lasting break in Southern racial practices. It has been said that the South was once bought by the Northern capitalists, who did not care much for the Negroes and allowed the Southerners almost complete freedom in the pursuit of any kind of racial discrimination. *Now Washington is the main "buyer" of the South.* And Washington usually seeks to extend its assistance regardless of race (463–464).

The New Deal did little for blacks formally and directly. But by establishing national programs of welfare, social security, public housing, public employment, and special programs for the rural poor, it directed aid toward Negroes,

North and South. Further, it indicated its sympathies by making black appointments, which had been few since Taft in Democratic and Republican administrations alike. Roosevelt's opposition to Hitler implied opposition to racist policies. Finally, important public actions came, though not without the pressure of organized blacks. In 1941, threatened with a "March on Washington" organized by black trade union leader A. Philip Randolph, the president issued an executive order banning discrimination in employment in defense industries or government, and setting up a Committee on Fair Employment Practices to enforce it. This was the first use of a major new tool, the executive order, to combat discrimination. National legislation remained impossible because of the power of southerners in Congress. The courts were cautious and slow. But the president could act independently. The model of an agency which could investigate complaints of discrimination, conduct hearings on them, and mobilize public opinion against discrimination, was established. Although the Fair Employment Practices Committee lapsed after the war, every president after Roosevelt maintained or expanded through executive order the federal obligation to ensure nondiscrimination in the federal civil service and among those who provided goods and services to the government. Under these orders the requirement of affirmative action by federal contractors eventually became in the late 1960s a powerful tool not only against discrimination in employment but also in moving toward proportional representation of racial and ethnic groups as a test of nondiscrimination.

The armed forces in World War II would seem to have been an obvious arena in which to institute policies of nondiscrimination. There blacks had either been excluded or limited to segregated and menial tasks. Although many branches of the armed forces were for the first time opened to blacks, segregation in both training and action remained the norm. But in 1948 President Truman issued an executive order calling for a policy of equal treatment and opportunity, and by implication the end of segregation. As in the case of the executive order against discrimination in government employment and among federal contractors, the fight against discrimination and segregation in the armed forces was to be a long one, but under executive pressure during and after the Korean War the armed forces became one of the most integrated institutions in American society.

Thus the New Deal and war generated actions beyond symbolism; yet in many crucial areas there was no action at all. Education remained strictly segregated in the South and in large parts of the rest of the country. Housing, despite the provision of public housing for blacks through federally subsidized action, remained segregated, including most public housing. Although both national parties called for a permanent FEPC in 1944, although President Truman urged it, and although distinguished presidential committees called for it, Congress would not act. In the post–World War II years as in the post-Reconstruction years, northern state governments took the lead in attacking discrimination in employment and education.

State Action
against Discrimination

In World War I blacks had begun to move north and west to escape southern segregation and violence and to find employment in industry. This migration continued in the 1920s, declined slightly in the 1930s, and was accelerated by World War II and the postwar mechanization of southern agriculture. The growth of Negro voting blocs in the North and West began to make blacks a significant force in national politics in the 1940s and increased their power in the states in which they had settled in substantial numbers. This migration was one of the causes of the proliferation of antidiscrimination laws in the northern states in the late 1940s. In this development blacks also had the strong support of the labor movement and of white ethnic groups, in particular

Jews, who also suffered from discrimination in employment, education, and housing.

The creation of state commissions to enforce nondiscriminatory practices set an important precedent for federal programs in the 1960s. These commissions were administrative agencies whose systematic proceedings were much more effective in combating discriminatory practices than were prosecutions of isolated civil or criminal suits under existing antidiscrimination statutes. The expense of the investigation was paid by the government and speedy action was taken by special agents upon receipt of a verified complaint. The burden of proof shifted to the party suspected of discriminatory acts. No jury was involved; instead an administrative board of experts determined the extent of discrimination and damages. Their authority was sufficiently broad so that they had the right to decide when "subterfuge or evasion" within the letter of the law was practiced.

In 1945 New York established the first state commission and the first permanent governmental agency designed to eradicate racial discrimination in employment. New York had been an early leader in this cause; 13 states had passed laws before 1945 prohibiting racial discrimination in certain occupations, but New York surpassed all the others in the comprehensiveness of its laws. As early as 1909 New York banned discrimination in the certification of lawyers; in 1918 it prohibited discrimination in any form of "state employment"; in 1933 the state outlawed discriminatory hiring practices by utility companies. Discriminatory practices by a labor union were prohibited in 1940 and were outlawed the next year in firms "engaged in defense work."

A coalition of white ethnic reformers, labor unions of the CIO, and black civil rights leaders secured the passage of the Ives-Quinn Bill of 1945, which established the New York agency for the maintenance of fair employment practices. Overwhelming majorities in the state senate and assembly passed the law against strong lobbying opposition, and it became a model for other states.

The bill created a State Commission Against Discrimination to eliminate and to prevent discriminatory practices by private employers, labor organizations, and employment agencies. It declared that employment without discrimination was a fundamental civil right. The commission was empowered to investigate complaints, to persuade accused parties to end discriminatory practices voluntarily, to hold formal hearings, and to issue cease-and-desist orders enforceable by court injunction. The commission monitored patterns of employment by keeping elaborate statistical records and made regular surveys of various employment fields. It also regularly conducted educational programs and issued literature encouraging employers to maintain fair hiring practices.

The activities of the commission brought the individual decisions of hiring, promoting, or dismissing employees, formerly considered wholly private, within the domain of actions reviewable by government, and introduced the concept that the duty of government was to engage in continuous supervision, intervention, and enforcement to ensure equality of access to employment.

Other states adopted similar laws: New Jersey in 1945; Massachusetts in 1946; Connecticut in 1947; New Mexico, Oregon, Rhode Island, and Washington in 1949; Pennsylvania, Michigan, and Minnesota in 1955; Wisconsin and Colorado in 1957; Ohio, Alaska, and California in 1959; and Delaware in 1960 all established fair employment commissions which incorporated the essential features of the original New York State Commission Against Discrimination.

Opinions as to the effectiveness of these efforts differed. But thousands of complaints were filed, many individuals received satisfaction, and patterns of employment began to change. Thus, in the later 1950s and 1960s one could see blacks employed in New York and other states in white-collar jobs in banks and insurance companies, as salesclerks in downtown department stores, and in other occupations where previously blacks had not been seen. Change was definitely on the way.

In 1948 New York extended the administrative procedure for ending discrimination to the field of education. The state commissioner of education was vested with powers to enforce fair educational practices by the same procedures as the State Commission Against Discrimination—investigation, conciliation, and administrative hearings. He was given an important additional power—the right to initiate an investigation if he had "reason to believe" that an institution had exercised any form of discrimination either against a single applicant or "against applicants as a group." New Jersey again followed New York's lead. By the late 1950s four more states—Massachusetts, Oregon, Pennsylvania, and Washington—had provided similar administrative protection for equal educational opportunity.

Access to housing had been seriously restricted by racial discrimination, and it was slower to receive the protection of state law. Connecticut in 1949 placed public housing within the purview of its fair employment commission and added publicly assisted housing in 1953. In 1955 the Connecticut commission was empowered to initiate an investigation whenever it had "reason to believe" that housing discrimination had occurred. By 1957 seven other states had placed public and publicly assisted housing under the jurisdiction of administrative agencies. Several states also prohibited discrimination in housing that received financial guarantees from the Federal Housing Administration and the Veterans Administration.

The rapid proliferation of state agencies that investigated, supervised, and enforced nondiscrimination in employment, education, and housing signified a transformation of the relationship between private rights and state responsibility for the civil welfare of all races. The establishment of these agencies expressed growing acceptance of the idea that state action against discriminatory practices was a legitimate exercise of police power to protect the welfare of the people, even when that power conflicted with the private control of property, education, and employment.

Court and Congress
Reenter the Field

Change in the South was barely perceptible; lynching declined, but massive segregation and the effective denial of political participation remained unbroken. But racism was no longer respectable in the aftermath of World War II, which had been fought against nations espousing racist doctrines. Anti-Semitism rapidly lost respectability. Anti-Chinese and anti-Japanese sentiment did not long survive World War II. The Chinese had been U.S. allies, and even though Japanese Americans had been interned in detention camps in World War II without regard to citizenship, and had been deprived of their property, anti-Japanese sentiment also surprisingly went into a rapid decline.

The decline in racist sentiment was evidenced in the revision of the immigration act in 1952. Asian nations, excluded by federal legislation in 1917 and 1924, now received minimal quotas. It appeared that the massive system of oppression in the South could not last, but the power of southern congressmen was great, for seniority gave them key committee chairmanships. The presidency, particularly under Democratic tenure, was responsive to black voting power in the North and to the strong support given to anti-discrimination measures by organized labor and white ethnics. But it could not make its recommendations effective in Congress.

Under these circumstances the task of destroying the southern racial system devolved on the federal courts. Many decisions before 1954 showed the Supreme Court was moving against segregation and discrimination; it had repeatedly struck down southern state legislation which in effect denied blacks the vote. In 1948 in *Shelley* v. *Kramer* it banned racially restrictive covenants that denied blacks and other groups the right to buy property. Important decisions in the field of professional higher education opened up opportunities to blacks; and in *Brown* v. *Board of Education of Topeka, Kansas* in 1954 the Supreme Court overturned *Plessy* and declared that in public education separate was inherently unequal, thus moving in on a key area of state action previously immune to federal intervention.

Dismantling school segregation in the South was no simple task, as the Supreme Court was well aware. It called only for "deliberate speed." The Court had directed that the system by which millions of students were taught, hundreds of thousands of teachers and administrators were employed, thousands of school districts were administered, must be changed. But there was a resounding silence from President Eisenhower. Nor did Congress act, except that a large group of southern legislators declared that the Court's decision was "an unwarranted exercise of power . . . contrary to the Constitution."

Some progress was rapid. Four states (Kansas, Arizona, New Mexico, and Wyoming) had permitted racial segregation only under local option, and they quickly changed their laws. Five states—Kentucky, Maryland, Missouri, Oklahoma, and West Virginia—and the District of Columbia swiftly eliminated state laws requiring segregation. The ten states of the Deep South resisted through legal maneuvers which were struck down by the courts. The president was forced to act in 1957 when Arkansas tried to prevent integration in Little Rock, but the executive branch left it to private litigators and overburdened courts to achieve the concrete steps to desegregation. But it would be impossible for the federal courts alone to restructure southern society, even though in the wake of *Brown* they struck down segregation in action after action, in field after field. The forces of Congress and the executive would have to be brought to bear.

The legal maneuvers of the NAACP and the NAACP Legal Defense Fund were supplemented in late 1955 by the sudden explosion of grassroots black protest. A boycott of the segregated buses in Montgomery, Ala., began spontaneously in 1955. Martin Luther King, Jr., a young minister, became its spokesman, received national publicity, and emerged as a popular and charismatic leader. In 1957, for the first time since 1875, the U.S. Congress passed civil rights legislation. It was more symbolic than effective, but it created a permanent and independent Civil Rights Commission to conduct investigations and issue reports, and authorized the attorney general to act against those who deprived people of the right to vote in federal elections.

Black protest continued, and the right to vote was still denied, particularly by the discriminatory use of literacy tests. In 1960 a black student "sit-in" movement rapidly spread. The Civil Rights Act of 1960 went further: the attorney general could ask a court to find a "pattern or practice" of voting-rights denial, and if it made such a finding, any individual otherwise qualified by the state law could apply to the court to order that he be allowed to vote. This, too, was without significant effect.

When in 1960 John F. Kennedy was elected president with heavy Negro support, it was hoped and expected that the executive would be drawn more actively into the battle against segregation and discrimination, but the new administration moved cautiously. In 1962 and 1963, when the governors of Mississippi and Alabama sought to deny blacks admission to their state universities, Kennedy did act forcefully. The black protest movement continued, demanding access to public accommodations and to the vote as its chief objectives, and reaching a climax in televised acts of nonviolent protest met by southern brutality in 1963. That year President Kennedy called for comprehensive civil rights legislation to end discrimination in public facilities and segregation in public schools and to increase the power of the federal government to protect the right to vote. The year 1963, the hundredth anniversary of Lincoln's Emancipation Proclamation, seemed a fitting time finally to achieve equality for blacks. In 1964, under the shock of Kennedy's assassination and with the strong support of President Lyndon B. Johnson, Congress passed the most farreaching Civil Rights Act. It was titled "An act to enforce the constitutional right to vote, to authorize the Attorney General to institute suits to protect constitutional rights in public facilities and public education, to extend the Commission on Civil Rights, to prevent discrimination in federally assisted programs, to establish a Commission on Equal Employment Opportunity, and for other purposes."

Title I of this legislation expanded the power of the attorney general to act to guarantee the right to vote; it was rapidly superseded in 1965 by the Voting Rights Act, which suspended any literacy test or other device to prevent voting in any jurisdiction in which less than 50 percent of the voting-age population had voted or registered in the presidential election of 1964. This act covered seven southern states; without design, it turned out also to cover some counties in the North. Finally the long resistance to black exercise of the suffrage was broken, and blacks in substantial numbers began to vote in the Deep South, changing its political composition and orientation.

Title II of the Civil Rights Act of 1964 barred discrimination in places of public accommodation and gave the attorney general the right to act against such discrimination. It was remarkably and rapidly effective in the deep South. Title III desegregated all facilities maintained by public organizations; again the attorney general was empowered to support and institute suits against such practices, and segregation fell rapidly. Title IV banned segregation in public education, with similar powers given to the attorney general. Title V extended the powers of the Civil Rights Commission. Title VI prohibited discrimination in any federally assisted program. Title VII outlawed discrimination in employment on grounds of race, color, sex, or national origin and established an Equal Employment Opportunities Commission. It could record complaints, investigate, and conciliate, but enforcement had to be referred to the attorney general.

The act was enormously effective. One of the reasons for its effectiveness was that simultaneously the federal government was expanding rapidly, providing grants to cities, states, and school districts, establishing new programs for the poor and expanding health care and higher education programs. Because almost every employer, every institution, and every branch of local and state government had become the beneficiary of federal funds, the capacity of the federal government to obtain compliance with nondiscrimination and nonsegregation through the threat of the cutting off of funds under Title VI was highly effective.

By the use of this power the long-drawn-out effort to achieve desegregation of southern schools finally succeeded. In 1968 the Supreme Court declared in *Green* v. *New Kent County* that a simple "freedom of choice" plan would not be enough to meet the mandate of *Brown* that schools be desegregated, because whites would not choose formerly black schools, and few blacks chose white schools. Using the power of Title VI of the Civil Rights Act, the Department of Health, Education, and Welfare required that specific percentages of black students in formerly white schools be reached in hundreds of southern districts. Despite the election of President Nixon, who was cool to the measures required for massive desegregation, by 1971 southern schools had become the most integrated in the United States.

But in the larger towns and cities schools were segregated wholly or in part because of black residential concentration. Nor was this a problem of the South alone; it was an even more serious problem in the North and West, where blacks were more heavily concentrated in large cities and black residential areas were much larger.

In 1971 the Supreme Court ruled unanimously in *Swann* v. *Mecklenburg County* that Charlotte, N.C., had to bus schoolchildren to overcome the vestiges of segregation. But Charlotte, like northern cities, had segregated schools because its black population was residentially concentrated and because, under the mandate of the *Brown* decision, it no longer assigned students to schools by race, but on the basis of where they lived. Such was the argument of the Charlotte school officials and of many northern districts that came under attack for school segregation.

The situation dealt with in the *Brown* decision—that in which state law required segregation and local school districts under official policy rigidly separated the races for education—had come to an end. But segregation in the schools as the result of residential concentration now came under criticism. An increasing number of plaintiffs attacking neighborhood school assignment tried to show that black concentrations in the schools were the result of local school-board actions, and thus state action, and not the result of residential concentration. When they succeeded, requirements to bus were imposed.

With the Civil Rights Act, a number of different powers became available to the federal government to fight discrimination in employment. The new Equal Employment Opportunity Commission (EEOC) turned out to have more extensive powers than the bare language of the act suggested. For example, the EEOC could issue regulations determining what was a discriminatory test of employment, and this power, within limits, was accepted by the Supreme Court in the *Griggs* case (1971). Thus, under certain circumstances the use of an intelligence test or the requirement that employees hold high-school diplomas could be considered discriminatory. The EEOC could require major corporations to adopt programs to hire given numbers of minorities and women, and to award back pay to minorities and women, by the threat of bringing action demonstrating discrimination (for example, the use of tests which it had declared discriminatory). Thus, the American Telephone and Telegraph Company accepted a consent judgment in 1972 requiring broad remedial actions to increase the number of higher-level minority and female employees. In 1972 the powers of the

Equal Employment Opportunity Commission were extended, even though by that time there was widespread concern that it was requiring "reverse discrimination"—the hiring and promotion of minorities (and women, who were also protected under the Civil Rights Act of 1964) over better qualified nonminority applicants and employees. Independent of the EEOC, but with substantial powers to affect the employment and promotion policies of employers, was the Office of Federal Contract Compliance. This federal agency operated under the authority of an executive order that required "affirmative action" to overcome discrimination by federal contractors. Under its regulations federal contractors were required to set "goals" for the hiring and promotion of given numbers of minority and female employees within a given time, in order to overcome "underutilization." With the expansion of federal spending programs, more and more employers came under the category of "federal contractors." Federally supported construction projects were the first to be brought under statistical hiring requirements under affirmative action, but the practice soon was required of other federal contractors, among them universities, and was soon adopted by many states and cities for their own contractors.

In addition, federal regulatory bodies such as the Federal Communications Commission also could act against discrimination, either under statute or under their own regulations, in the industries they regulated. Individuals who encountered discrimination now had many options—state law, the civil rights act, and federal regulations; they could sue also under the old Reconstruction civil rights statutes, resuscitated by the federal courts. Overt, direct discrimination rapidly became an anachronism, and the more difficult question that replaced it was, what was discrimination? Were union seniority rules discrimination under the law? Were tests which selected different proportions of minority groups discrimination under the law? And were affirmative action plans designed to increase the proportions of minorities discrimination against whites under the law? These were the issues that began to emerge in the late 1960s and were still unsettled in the late 1970s.

The 1970s: Beyond Discrimination

In the middle and late 1960s, as blacks rioted in American cities, as Mexican-Americans and Puerto Ricans became politically active, as American Indians for the first time entered the arena of national politics, and as white ethnic groups also became more assertive—both in reaction to black political action, and to foster aims of their own, such as establishing the legitimacy of the maintenance of their cultures and languages—the American polity seemed to be engaged in a massive effort finally to put problems of racial and ethnic discrimination behind it. Thus, in 1965 the Hart-Celler Immigration Act swept away quotas based on race and national origin, and in 1968 a fair-housing act banned racial and ethnic discrimination.

But although segregated education by law became obsolete, and black employment rose in professional and white-collar occupations and in skilled labor, the problem of ending discrimination against racial and minority groups was not removed from the agenda of public life. Discrimination as it had been understood until the middle 1960s declined rapidly, but new issues that had not previously been considered under the heading of discrimination now emerged.

Some of these new problems arose in education and employment. Northern cities which had not thought of themselves as doing so were found by judges to have practiced segregation, enough to require the massive remedy of busing of schoolchildren so as to approximate in each school the proportions of children by race in the school district. Busing thus came to San Francisco, Boston, Denver, and other cities, generally with considerable conflict, for it infringed on the traditional neighborhood school. Whites left the cities in which black schoolchildren increased in number, and in which busing was instituted. A fierce dispute erupted over the causes of "white flight," but whatever the reasons, it was clear that blacks were becoming the majority population in more and more cities. Should then central cities be joined with suburbs to permit higher proportions of whites in urban schools? The Supreme Court denied such a solution in Detroit, permitted it in Louisville, Ky., and Wilmington, Del. Congress, which had acted so forcefully in 1964, now withdrew from defining standards of desegregation, except for the passage of occasional antibusing amendments which bound the federal bureaucracy but were without effect in the courts. The courts acted erratically; even the Supreme Court's standards became obscure, and on similar facts some federal courts imposed busing and others did not.

Behind this new, confused, and complex situation lay the reality of poor black achievement in schools. Would integration improve their scores? Would it improve them if it were imposed on unwilling whites? Could enough whites be induced to stay in the cities in which such drastic measures were adopted? While to parents the educational issues were undoubtedly paramount, to the litigants trying to prove segregation, and to the judges who accepted these proofs, it was doubtful whether the ultimate aim of improved education carried much weight against what they conceived as a moral, constitutional, and social imperative. To parents and the public at large, busing raised the contradictory picture of federal agencies requiring assignment to schools on the basis of race and ethnic group, now to achieve integration rather than segregation.

In the later 1960s and 1970s new dimensions were added to the issue of discrimination in education as Spanish-American and Asian-American groups became active. For them the problem of education was less one of segregation—to which they had also, in one degree or another, been subject —than of the attitude of public school authorities toward their language and culture. Public schools typically had ignored the foreign-language background of children; they had not taken into account the difficulties this background created for education in English. In addition, they often actively suppressed the use of foreign languages by schoolchildren. Many Mexican-American and Puerto Rican leaders wanted public schools to acknowledge that foreign-language background required special programs. Others went further: they wanted public schools to encourage the maintenance of foreign-language ability and to teach children of their ethnic group something of their group's culture. To some extent these paralleled black demands for black studies in the public schools.

But inevitably demands for special programs designed for children of a given ethnic group—whether these programs facilitated the teaching of English, or maintained language competence and cultural knowledge—conflicted with the demands for desegregation and integration. Should children of a given ethnic group be scattered, as in the pattern developing for black children, or be concentrated so that they could be educated in their own language and culture?

Even where this conflict was not severe, these new demands ran counter to what those fighting discrimination had originally set as their objective. Antidiscrimination legislation had been written under the assumption that public policy should be blind to race and ethnic group. Representatives of minority groups now demanded that public policy be responsive to the specific culture of each ethnic group. In 1968 federal legislation provided funds for bilingual programs. In 1974 this legislation was amended to expand the type and level of federal support for bilingual and bicultural education programs, including full-scale bilingual and bicultural education programs as an end in themselves rather than solely as a vehicle for easing the transition to English-only education.

Further, in 1974 the Supreme Court in its *Lau* decision upheld regulations of the Office of Civil Rights of the Department of Health, Education, and Welfare requiring bilingual programs for students of limited English-language ability. The Office of Civil Rights had interpreted the prohibition of discrimination in educational programs on grounds of national origin in the Civil Rights Act of 1964 as requiring this kind of response to language problems of students. As a result, school districts were both required to provide bilingual-bicultural education by the Office of Civil Rights, and were assisted in doing so by federal legislation. This was only one of the ways in which the long fight against discrimination shifted, in the early 1970s, to demanding public action that was conscious of, rather than blind to, color and ethnic group.

In the field of employment, "affirmative action" became the issue. It was required under executive orders which governed contracts with federal contractors. It was demanded increasingly by the EEOC, the attorney general, and federal courts in cases where discrimination could be proved. And it was increasingly accepted by business, nonprofit, and public employers, either because they were federal contractors or because they knew that under EEOC regulations their employment practices could be shown to be discriminatory (for example, if they used tests with disproportionate impact), even though they had not discriminated intentionally. Race and ethnicity became key factors in estimating eligibility for a job or a promotion, not in order to keep blacks and Spanish-surnamed Americans down, but to raise them up. But this meant taking account of race and ethnic background. In 1964 all sides seemed agreed that color and ethnicity should be of no account in education and employment, and it was assumed and expected that what was intended by the legislation of that day was color-blind, not color-conscious, public policy. Color consciousness, however, became the accepted public policy in the 1970s, not through congressional action—Congress on the whole still opposed it—but through the actions of permanent agencies that had been established to administer and enforce the anti-discrimination laws, and through the agreement of the courts with the way in which they carried out their mandate. In the view of many, however, these agencies were subverting the very laws they were supposed to enforce.

"Reverse discrimination" thus became the issue of the later 1970s. Strangely, it was cases in the field of higher education that brought it most prominently to public attention. First, Marco DeFunis, a Jewish applicant to the University of Washington Law School, sued the school when he was not admitted because it had a program favoring the admission of minorities. The Supreme Court refused to rule on the case, but it was clear that it was deeply divided. Then Allan Bakke, a white, filed suit because he was not admitted to the medical school of the University of California at Davis, which also had a program favoring the admission of minorities. Such practices were common in law and medical schools, where action to increase the number of minorities was widespread. The *Bakke* case spurred a passionate national debate on the problem of affirmative action and reverse discrimination. The debate divided old allies in the struggles for civil rights; the sharpest and most poignant division was between black and Jewish civil rights organizations, which had been closely allied for 30 years in achieving state and national antidiscrimination legislation. The Supreme Court in 1978 ruled on the *Bakke* case, but it was more divided than it had been for decades on a civil rights issue. Four justices would have upheld quotas, four would have rejected them under Title VI of the Civil Rights Act of 1964, and only one, writing a complex decision, permitted the Court to issue a complex and ambiguous judgment in favor of Bakke.

The decision marked a strong contrast with the unanimous ruling in *Brown* and in civil rights cases for almost 20 years following. It reflected a divided country. But it reflected, too, the end of the long history of overt discrimination against minorities as a major theme in American history. There was now a new issue: what kind of positive action in favor of minorities was to be accepted as legitimate and constitutional?

BIBLIOGRAPHY

1. Prejudice

Gordon Allport, *The Nature of Prejudice* (Reading, Mass., 1954) remains the definitive psychological treatment of the subject. More recent discussions that update Allport's analysis include: John Harding, Harold Proshansky, Bernard Kutner, and Isidor Chein, "Prejudice and Ethnic Relations," in *The Handbook of Social Psychology*, 2d ed., vol. 5, ed. Gardner Lindzey and Elliot Aronson (Reading, Mass., 1969); and Thomas Pettigrew, *Racially Separate or Together?* (New York, 1971). A modern psychoanalytic analysis of anti-black prejudice is Joel Kovel, *White Racism: A Psychohistory* (New York, 1970). Four primary sources of psychological research on prejudice are particularly noteworthy and readable: T. W. Adorno, E. Frenkel-Brunswik, D. J. Levinson, and R. N. Sanford, *The Authoritarian Personality* (New York, 1950); Judith Porter, *Black Child, White Child* (Cambridge, Mass., 1971); John Williams and J. Kenneth Morland, *Race, Color, and the Young Child* (Chapel Hill, N.C., 1976); and Phyllis Katz, ed., *Towards the Elimination of Racism* (New York, 1976).

Outstanding sociological treatments of the subject are provided in George Simpson and J. Milton Yinger, *Racial and Cultural Minorities*, 4th ed. (New York, 1972); and Robin Williams, Jr., *Strangers Next Door* (Englewood Cliffs, N.J., 1964). The classic analysis of black-white relations in the United States is Gunnar Myrdal, *An American Dilemma* (New York, 1944). A collection of recent sociological analyses of American race relations is found in Thomas F. Pettigrew, ed., *Racial Discrimination in the United States* (New York, 1975). An overview of the sociological study of race relations since 1895 is presented in Thomas F. Pettigrew, ed., *The Sociology of Race Relations: Reflection and Reform* (New York, 1980). A range of brief and authoritative articles can be found in David Sills, ed., *The International Encyclopedia of the Social Sciences* (New York, 1968); see especially articles on aggression, anti-Semitism, attitudes, attitude change, conformity, minorities, prejudice, race, race relations, social discrimination, and stereotypes.

2. A History of Discrimination

A conceptual scheme for understanding the historical roots of prejudice and discrimination is suggested by Donald L. Noel, "A Theory of the Origin of Ethnic Stratification," *Social Problems* 16 (1968): 157– 172. Thomas F. Gossett, *Race: The History of an Idea in America* (1963; reprint, New York, 1968), surveys a principal intellectual rationale for ethnic inequality. Many insights into how both blacks and white immigrants were viewed and treated can be found in Oscar Handlin, *Race and Nationality in American Life* (Boston, 1957). A competent overview of white attitudes toward American Indians is Robert F. Berkhofer, Jr., *The White Man's Indian* (New York, 1978). Another valuable treatment of the same subject is Roy Harvey Pearce, *The Savages of America: A Study of the Indian and the Idea of Civilization* (Baltimore, 1953). On prejudice and discrimination against blacks in early American history, see Winthrop D. Jordan's monumental *White over Black: American Attitudes toward the Negro, 1550–1812* (Chapel Hill, N.C., 1968). Two important studies that deal with the later evolution of antiblack attitudes and policies are George M. Fredrickson, *The Black Image in the White Mind: The Debate on Afro-American Character and Destiny, 1817–1914* (New York, 1971), and C. Vann Woodward, *The Strange Career of Jim Crow*, 3d rev. ed. (New York, 1974). Gunnar Myrdal, *An American Dilemma: The Negro Problem and Modern Democracy* (1944; reprint, New York, 1975), contains a vast amount of material on discrimination against Afro-Americans before World War II. On prejudice and discrimination against Asian Americans, see three recent works: Stuart Creighton Miller, *The Unwelcome Immigrant: The American Image of the Chinese, 1785–1882* (Berkeley, Calif., 1969); Alexander Saxton, *The Indispensable Enemy: Labor and the Anti-Chinese Movement in California* (Berkeley, 1971); and Roger Daniels, *The Politics of Prejudice: The Anti-Japanese Movement in California and the Struggle for Japanese Exclusion* (Berkeley, 1962). There are no major scholarly studies dealing comprehensively with the history of prejudice and discrimination against Spanish-speaking Americans, but Carey McWilliams, *North from Mexico* (1948; reprint, New York, 1968), remains valuable. The standard work on Anglo-American nativism is still John Higham, *Strangers in the Land: Patterns of American Nativism, 1860–1925* (New York, 1963). Higham's later reflections on this subject along with a more extensive account of anti-Semitism can be found in *Send These to Me: Jews and Other Immigrants in Urban America* (New York, 1975). Oscar Handlin, *Boston's Immigrants, 1790–1880: A Study in Acculturation*, rev. ed. (New York, 1972), is the standard treatment of ethnocultural and socioeconomic conflict in the northeastern United States before the Civil War. Edward Digby Baltzell, *The Protestant Establishment: Aristocracy and Caste in America* (New York, 1964), describes recent manifestations of elite discrimination against members of white ethnic groups.

3.   Efforts against Prejudice

The most informative historical studies of state and municipal action in the 19th century are Leonard Levy and Harlan B. Phillips, "The Roberts Case: Source of the 'Separate but Equal' Doctrine," *American Historical Review* 56 (1951): 510–518, and Leon Litwack, *North of Slavery* (Chicago, 1961). Morton Keller, *Affairs of State* (Cambridge, Mass., 1977), provides a thoughtful overview of civil rights legislation and the changing status of blacks after the Civil War. J. R. Pole, *The Pursuit of Equality in American History* (Berkeley, Calif., 1978), is a survey of legal and constitutional ideas about the nature of equality in American society.

Several works by legal scholars are informative on the constitutional issues in the history of public policy against discrimination: Derrick A. Bell, Jr., *Race, Racism, and American Law* (Boston, 1973); Raoul Berger, *Government by Judiciary: The Transformation of the Fourteenth Amendment* (Cambridge, Mass., 1976); Jack Greenberg, *Race Relations and American Law* (New York, 1959); Milton Konvitz, *A Century of Civil Rights* (New York, 1961), and *The Constitution and Civil Rights* (1946; reprint, New York, 1977); and Bernard D. Reams, Jr. and Paul E. Wilson, *Segregation and the Fourteenth Amendment in the United States* (Buffalo, N.Y., 1975). Also helpful is Leon H. Mayhew, *Law and Equal Opportunity* (Cambridge, Mass., 1968).

The major work on the position of blacks at the beginning of World War II, with extensive analysis of policies imposing segregation and discriminatory treatment and the nascent efforts to counter legal and extralegal deprivation of the country's largest minority, is Gunnar Myrdal, *An American Dilemma* (New York, 1944). John Hope Franklin, *From Slavery to Freedom: A History of American Negroes* (New York, 1964), describes antidiscrimination policy in the postwar period. Albert P. Blaustein and Robert L. Zangrando, *Civil Rights and the American Negro: A Documentary History* (New York, 1968), chronicles the history of the civil rights movement and its major legal and legislative successes. Many books cover specific aspects of the legal counterattack on discrimination, among them Howard I. Kalodner and James J. Fishman, eds., *Limits of Justice: The Courts' Role in School Desegregation* (Cambridge, Mass., 1978); and Herbert Hill, *Black Labor and the American Legal System, Volume I* (Washington, D.C., 1977), which goes up to the end of World War II.

Lino A. Graglia, *Disaster by Decree: The Supreme Court Decisions on Race and the Schools* (Ithaca, N.Y., 1976), analyzes the major Supreme Court decisions and is critical of the most recent turn in favor of busing. Nathan Glazer, *Affirmative Discrimination: Ethnic Inequality and Public Policy* (New York, 1975), is also critical of this development, as well as of new developments of antidiscrimination law and regulation imposing statistical tests of nondiscrimination. The literature on "reverse discrimination" or "affirmative action" is voluminous. For a sampling see Barry Gross, ed., *Reverse Discrimination* (Buffalo, N.Y., 1977); John E. Fleming, Gerald R. Gill, and David H. Swinton, *The Case for Affirmative Action for Blacks in Higher Education* (Washington, D.C., 1978); and Allen P. Sindler, *Bakke, DeFunis and Minority Admissions: The Quest for Equal Opportunity* (New York, 1978).